MOON

Road Trip USA

Pacific Coast Highway

JAMIE JENSEN

AVALON
TRAVEL

CONTENTS

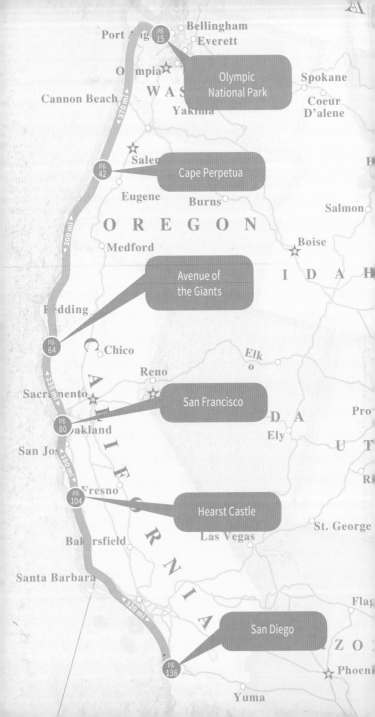

Bellingham
Port Ang 1g
Everett

pg. 15

Olympic National Park

Olympia

Spokane

CANNON BEACH

WAS

Coeur D'alene

Yakima

370 mi

Salem

pg. 42

Cape Perpetua

Eugene

Burns

Salmon

OREGON

Medford

Boise

IDAH

300 mi

Avenue of the Giants

Redding

pg. 64

Chico

Elk o

Reno

CA

235 mi

Sacramento

San Francisco

DA

pg. 80

Oakland

Ely

U   T

San Jos

180 mi

Fresno

pg. 104

Hearst Castle

Pro

R

St. George

Bakersfield

Las Vegas

RNIA

Santa Barbara

320 mi

Flag

San Diego

A

pg. 136

ZO

Phoeni

Yuma

Pacific Coast Highway

CALIFORNIA
1

The amazing thing about the West Coast is that it is still mostly wild, open, and astoundingly beautiful country, where you can drive for miles and miles and have the scenery all to yourself.

Between Olympic National Park and San Diego, California

For some reason, when people elsewhere in the country refer to the Pacific Coast, particularly **California**, it's apparent that they think it's a land of kooks and crazies, an overbuilt suburban desert supporting only shopping malls, freeways, and body-obsessed airheads. All this may be true in small pockets, but the amazing thing about the Pacific Coast—from the dense green forests of western **Washington** to the gorgeous beaches of Southern California—is that it is still mostly wild, open, and astoundingly beautiful country, where you can drive for miles and miles and have the scenery all to yourself.

Starting at the northwest tip of the United States at **Olympic National Park**, and remaining within sight of the ocean almost all the way south to the Mexican border, this 1,650-mile, mostly two-lane route takes in everything from temperate rainforest to near-desert. Most of the Pacific Coast is in the public domain, accessible, and protected from development within national, state, and local parks, which provide habitat for such rare creatures as mountain lions, condors, and gray whales.

Heading south, after the rough-and-tumble logging and fishing communities of Washington State, you cross the mouth of the Columbia River and follow the comparatively peaceful and quiet **Oregon** coastline, where recreation has by and large replaced industry, and where dozens of quaint and not-so-quaint communities line the ever-changing shoreline. At the midway point, you pass through the great redwood forests of Northern California, where the tallest and most majestic living things on earth line the "**Avenue of the Giants**," home also to some of the best (meaning gloriously kitsch) remnants of the golden age of car-borne tourism: drive-through trees, drive-on trees, houses carved out of trees, and much more. The phenomenally beautiful coastline of Northern California is rivaled only by the incredible coast of **Big Sur** farther south, beyond which stretch the beachfronts of Southern California. The land of palm trees, beach boys, and surfer girls of popular lore really does exist, though only in the southernmost quarter of the state.

Along with the overwhelming scale of its natural beauty, the West Coast is remarkable for the abundance of well-preserved historic sites—most of which haven't been torn down, built on, or even built around—that stand as vivid evocations of life on what was once the most distant frontier of the New World. While rarely as old as places on the East Coast, or as impressive as those in Europe, West Coast sites are quite diverse and include the Spanish colonial missions of California, Russian and English fur-trading outposts, and the place where Lewis and Clark first sighted the Pacific after their long slog across the continent.

Last but certainly not least are the energizing cities—**Seattle** and **Portland** in the north, **San Francisco** in the middle, and **Los Angeles** and **San Diego** to the south—which serve as gateways to (or civilized respites from) the landscapes in between them. Add to these the dozens of small and not-so-small towns along the coast, with alternating blue-collar ports and upscale vacation retreats, and you have a great range of food, drink, and accommodation options. Local cafés, seafood grills, and bijou restaurants abound, as do places to stay—from youth hostels in old lighthouses to roadside motels (including the world's first, which still stands in lovely San Luis Obispo, California) to homespun B&B inns in old farmhouses

Big Sur

WASHINGTON

The coast of Washington is a virtual microcosm of the Pacific Northwest, containing everything from extensive wilderness areas to Native American fishing villages and heavily industrialized lumber towns. Starting at splendid **Port Townsend,** US-101 loops west around the rugged Olympic Peninsula, passing near the northwesternmost point of the continental United States while allowing access to the unforgettable natural attractions—sandy, driftwood-strewn beaches; primeval old-growth forests; and pristine mountain lakes and glaciated alpine peaks, to name just a few—of **Olympic National Park.** The roadside landscape varies from dense woods to clear-cut tracts of recently harvested timber. Innumerable rivers and streams are perhaps the most obvious signs of the immense amount of rainfall (about 12 feet) the region receives every year. Scattered towns, from **Port Angeles** in the north to the twin cities of **Grays Harbor** on the coast, are staunchly blue-collar communities almost wholly dependent upon natural resources—not only trees, but also salmon, oysters, and other seafood. Though the tourism trade has been increasing steadily, visitor services are still few and far between, so plan ahead.

Though it's not on the ocean, the Puget Sound port city of **Seattle** makes a good starting or finishing point to this Pacific Coast road trip.

Port Townsend

Few places in the world can match the concentration of natural beauty or the wealth of architecture found in tiny **Port Townsend** (pop. 9,113). One of the oldest towns in Washington, Port Townsend was laid out in 1852 and reached a peak of activity in the 1880s. But after the railroads focused on Seattle and Puget Sound as their western terminus, the town sat quietly for most of the next century until the 1960s, when an influx of arts-oriented refugees took over the waterfront warehouses and cliff-top mansions, converting them to galleries, restaurants, and comfy B&Bs while preserving the town's turn-of-the-20th-century character.

Port Townsend is neatly divided into two halves: Multi-story brick warehouses and commercial buildings line Water Street and the wharves along the bay, while lovely old Victorian houses cover the bluffs above. It's basically a great place to wander, but there are

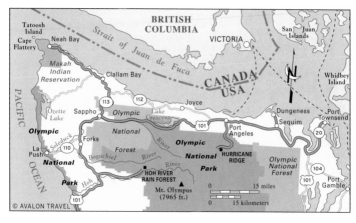

a couple of sights worth seeing, particularly the landmark **City Hall** (250 Madison St.) along the east end of Water Street. Half of this eclectic gothic pile now houses a local historical museum with two floors of odds and ends tracing Port Townsend history, including the old city jail where Jack London spent a night on his way to the Klondike goldfields in 1897.

On the north side of Port Townsend, **Fort Worden** is a retired military base that served as a location for the Richard Gere movie *An Officer and a Gentleman*. Now home to a wonderful natural history museum, the old fort also hosts an excellent series of annual music and arts festivals; contact local arts organization **Centrum** (360/385-3102) for schedules and more information.

Fort Worden

TOWARD SEATTLE: PORT GAMBLE

You have a number of options if traveling to or from Port Townsend. You can follow US-101 around the western Olympic Peninsula, or take a ferry via Whidbey Island and explore it and the even prettier San Juan Islands to the north. Last, but not least, you can take a middle route across the Kitsap Peninsula, then catch a ferry to **Seattle** (see page 12).

This last route, which includes a trip on the very frequent Washington State Ferries between Kingston and Edmonds, has the great advantage of taking you through **Port Gamble,** a slice of New England on the shores of Puget Sound. Owned and run by the Pope & Talbot Lumber Company from the 1850s until the mill shut down in 1995, the entire town is a National Historic Landmark District, with dozens of immaculate Victorian buildings standing along maple tree-lined streets. After wandering past the saltbox houses, have a look inside the large **Port Gamble General Store** (32400 NE Rainier Ave., 360/297-7636), which includes a seashell museum, a local history museum ($4), and a popular café.

Port Townsend Practicalities

Not surprisingly, considering the extensive tourist trade, Port Townsend has a number of good restaurants and bars. You'll find many of the best places at the east end of town near the corner of Water and Quincy Streets. For breakfast, try **Addie Mae's Southern Kitchen** (634 Water St., 360/385-1236) or the water-front **Point Hudson Cafe** (130 Hudson St., 360/379-0592), at the far east end of downtown "PT." For lunch or dinner, one of the best seafood places is the **Silverwater Cafe** (237 Taylor St., 360/385-6448), still going strong after 25 years near the Quincy Street dock. The old waterfront neighborhood also holds a pair of hotels in restored 1880s buildings: **The Waterstreet Hotel** (635 Water St., 360/385-5467 or 800/735-9810, $60 and up) and the quieter **The Palace Hotel** (1004 Water St., 360/385-

The natural cut of the **Hood Canal** on the east side of the Olympic Peninsula is one of the West Coast's prime oyster-growing estuaries, source of the gourmet Quilcenes, Hama Hamas, and other varieties available at roadside stands, shops, and restaurants throughout the region.

0773, $99 and up), where the room names play up the building's past use as a brothel.

The most comfortable accommodations in Port Townsend are the many 1880s-era B&Bs dotting the bluffs above the port area, including the ever-popular **The Old Consulate Inn** (313 Walker St., 360/385-6753, $110 and up), where some of the plush rooms come with a view of the Olympic Mountains and all come with a hearty multi-course breakfast.

Fort Worden State Park (360/344-4400), a mile north of downtown, also offers a wide variety of memorable accommodations in historic officers quarters and converted barracks.

Sequim and Dungeness

Forty minutes southwest of Port Town-send via Hwy-20 and US-101, **Sequim** (pop. 6,606; pronounced "SKWIM") sits in the rain shadow of the Olympic Mountains and so tends to be much drier and sunnier than spots even a few miles west. Though it retains its rural feel, Sequim's historic farming-and-fishing economy is quickly switching over to tourism, with tracts of new homes filling up the rolling, waterfront landscape and a new freeway bypassing the center of town. It's ideal cycling country, for the moment at least, with acres and acres of lavender farms lining quiet country roads.

Sequim lavender fields

Coming in from the east on two-lane US-101, the first thing you pass is the large, modern John Wayne Marina, built on land donated by The Duke's family. The US-101 frontage through town is lined by the usual franchised fast-food outlets and some unique variations, like the 1950s-themed **Hi Way 101 Diner** (392 W. Washington St., 360/683-3388), in the heart of town.

Just north of US-101, the **MAC Exhibit Center** (175 W. Cedar St., 360/683-8110, Tues.-Sat. 10am-3pm, $3) houses everything from 12,000-year-old mastodon bones discovered on a nearby farm

Sequim's annual **Irrigation Festival,** held every May, is Washington's oldest continuing community celebration. The **Lavender Festival,** in July, is also very popular.

The Native American-owned **7 Cedars Casino** stands above US-101 at the foot of Sequim Bay, fronted by totem poles.

Seattle

An engaging and energetic combination of scenic beauty, blue-collar grit, and high-tech panache has made Seattle one of the most popular cities in the United States, for visitors and residents alike. A young city, historically and demographically, Seattle has managed to preserve much of its heavy industrial heritage as parks and museums, if not as economic engines. The eco-conscious, civic-minded city spreads over a series of hills, surrounded by the waters of Puget Sound (be sure to ride a ferry or two!), with a backdrop of the snowcapped Cascade and Olympic Mountains. The evergreen Seattle can be an entrancing city—at least when the sun comes out, which no matter what people say is likely to happen at least once during your stay.

The heart of downtown Seattle, **Pike Place Market** is a raucous fish, crafts, and farmers market with some 500 different stalls and stores filling an early-1900s municipal-feeling building that steps along the waterfront. For a respite from the hubbub, head two blocks south to the postmodern **Seattle Art Museum** (1300 1st Ave., 206/654-3100, closed Mon. and Tues., $19.50) and enjoy the amazing collection of regional Native American art and artifacts on display. Downtown's other piece of noteworthy recent

Pike Place Market

architecture is the shiny **Seattle Central Library** (1000 4th Ave.), a fantastic (and free!) high-tech (some say hermetic) space whose multifaceted glass diamond exterior steps down between two city blocks.

At the south edge of downtown, a little under a mile from Pike Place Market, the 20-some-block **Pioneer Square** historic district preserves the original core of the city, which boomed in the late 1890s with the Klondike Gold Rush. Just south of Pioneer Square, spectators can enjoy downtown views and Puget Sound sunsets at Safeco Field ballpark, where the **Seattle Mariners** (206/346-5000) play. The soccer Sounders and NFL champion Seahawks play next door at CenturyLink Field, cheered on by the world's loudest fans (136+ decibels).

Another essential place to go is the **Seattle Center** (206/684-7200), a mile north of downtown at Broad Street and 5th Avenue North, built for the 1962 World's Fair, and featuring Seattle's Space Age icon, the **Space Needle** ($10-22). The Seattle Center, which you can reach via a quick ride on Seattle's short monorail, is the primary location for Seattle's excellent annual Labor Day arts and music festival, **Bumbershoot,** and is also home to the intriguing Experience Music Project, now better known as **EMP** (206/770-2700, daily, $18), a hands-on musical exploration that includes a living memorial to the city's native-born guitar genius, Jimi Hendrix. A don't-miss photo opportunity: a statue of Chief Seattle with the Space Needle rising behind him.

Besides funding EMP, Microsoft billionaire Paul Allen has indulged his taste for Space Age adventure by subsidizing the private rocket ship SpaceShipOne, and closer to home by renovating the widescreen **Cinerama theater** (2100 4th Ave., 206/448-6680), an early 1960s icon.

PRACTICALITIES

Seattle's main airport is Seattle-Tacoma International Airport ("Sea-Tac"), a half-hour drive south of downtown Seattle via the I-5 freeway. Seattle's freeways are often filled to capacity most of the day, but the best drive-through tour of Seattle follows old US-99 along the Alaskan Way Viaduct, a concrete freeway that cuts along the downtown water-front, runs through a tunnel, then follows Aurora Avenue on a soaring bridge over the west end of Lake Union. (By the way, under the Aurora Bridge sits one of Seattle's biggest pieces of auto-art: the **Fremont Troll,** caught in the act of capturing an old VW Beetle.)

Most everything of visitor interest in Seattle is within the walkably com-pact downtown, where an extensive bus system runs in a fare-free zone; there's also a 1.2-mile-long **monorail** ($2.25 one-way), linking 5th Avenue and Pine Street downtown with the Seattle Center and Space Needle.

The niftiest place to stay is the **Hotel Ändra** (2000 4th Ave., 206/448-8600, $189 and up), a fully modernized 1920s hotel just a short walk from Pike Place Market. At the other end of the scale, the cheapest place to stay has to be the newly renovated **HI-Seattle at the American Hotel** (520 S. King St., 206/622-5443, dorm beds around $30), just east of Pioneer Square, which offers clean and comfortable dorm beds.

Seafood, not surprisingly, is the thing Seattle restaurants do best, and the city is full of great places to eat fish. The sushi here is as good as it gets, outside Japan. Try **Maneki** (304 6th Ave. S., 206/622-2631), which has been serving fresh sushi for over 100 years in the International District. For fish-and-chips or cheap, fresh oysters (and Washington pro-duces more oysters than anywhere else in the United States), head down to **Emmett Watson's Oyster Bar** (206/448-7721) at the north end of Pike Place Market. More down-home fare is served up for breakfast, lunch, and dinner at the **5 Spot** (1502 Queen Anne Ave. N., 206/285-7768), in the residential Queen Anne district, about two miles northwest of downtown high above Lake Union.

The best source of advance information on visiting Seattle is **Seattle's Convention and Visitors Bureau** (206/461-5840).

to exhibits of Native American cultures and pioneer farm implements. From the museum, a well-marked road winds north for 7 miles before reaching the waterfront again at **Dungeness,** where a 5.5-mile-long sand spit, the country's longest, protects a shellfish-rich wildlife refuge.

Cyclists and kayakers in particular like to stay near Sequim at the waterfront **Juan de Fuca Cottages** (182 Marine Dr., 360/683-4433, $160 and up), across from Dungeness Bay on a peaceful road about seven miles northwest of town.

Port Angeles

A busy, industrial city at the center of the northern Olympic Peninsula, **Port Angeles** (pop. 19,038) makes a handy base for visiting the nearby wilderness of Olympic National Park. The town is slowly but surely recovering from its traditional dependence on logging, and the waterfront, which once hummed to the sound of lumber and pulp mills, is now bustling with tourists wandering along a 6.5-mile walking trail and enjoying the sea life (sea slugs, starfish, and octopuses) on display at the small but enjoyable **Feiro Marine Life Center** (daily 10am-5pm during summer, daily noon-4pm during off-season, $4 adults), on the centrally located Port Angeles City Pier.

OLYMPIC NATIONAL PARK

Olympic National Park, in the heart of the Olympic Peninsula, is a diversely beautiful corner of the country, combining features of Maine's rocky coast and the snowcapped peaks of the Rocky Mountains with the unique rainforests covering the park's Pacific coastal valleys. The rugged, nearly million-acre landscape, ranging from rocky shores to impassably dense forests, resisted exploitation and development until the turn of the 20th century, when local conservationists persuaded Teddy Roosevelt to declare much of the peninsula a national monument, a movement that eventually resulted in the establishment of Olympic National Park in 1938.

There are no roads and few trails across the peninsula, so you have to choose your points of entry depending upon what you want to see. The different areas of Olympic National Park are covered in the surrounding pages, but the most popular part of the park is Hurricane Ridge, which rises high above Port Angeles and offers great views of the silvery peaks and the many glaciers that flank them. (The wildflowers can be spectacular in late spring.)

At the northwestern corner of the park, Lake Crescent sits serenely amidst the forests and peaks, while on the western slopes, the temperate rainforests of the usually wet and rainy river valleys hold some of the world's largest trees, all draped with a thick fabric of mosses. At the western edge of the peninsula, the almost completely undeveloped Pacific Ocean coastline, added to the park in 1953, offers miles of sandy beaches and rocky headlands, littered only with driftwood logs and vibrant tide pools.

Malls, gas stations, and fast-food franchises line the US-101 frontage through town, but life in Port Angeles, for locals and visitors alike, centers on the attractive downtown area, two blocks inland from the waterfront around Lincoln Street and 1st Street. Here cafés like **First Street Haven** (107 E. 1st St., 360/457-0352) offer great breakfasts and good yet inexpensive soup-and-salad lunches, while amiable bars and pubs draw bikers, hikers, and loggers with their pub grub and good beers (more than 50 bottles, plus some in-

The old-growth forests of **Olympic National Park** provide prime habitat for the northern spotted owl, an endangered species whose preservation has sparked heated debate throughout the Pacific Northwest.

FERRIES TO VICTORIA, BRITISH COLUMBIA

From Port Angeles, the **Black Ball Ferry Line** (360/457-4491, around $60 per car and driver one-way, plus $17.50 per additional person) carries cars and passengers, shuttling across the water to and from pretty Victoria, the provincial capital of British Columbia, one of Canada's most popular destinations. Ships leave Port Angeles at the middle of the attractively landscaped waterfront and arrive very near the center of Victoria, making for a great day trip from either place. At the Port Angeles dock there's a very helpful information center packed with maps and brochures on Victoria and the rest of B.C., or you can call **Tourism Victoria** (800/663-3883).

triguing "home brews"). If you're waiting for a boat, or are fresh off of one, more places to eat and drink surround the ferry terminal.

Places to stay in Port Angeles vary. You'll find highway motels, including the **Quality Inn Uptown** (101 E. 2nd St., 360/457-9434, $85 and up), and the **Red Lion Hotel** (360/452-9215, $119 and up), on the water at the foot of Lincoln Street. There are also many characterful B&Bs.

Hurricane Ridge

High above Port Angeles, **Hurricane Ridge** provides the most popular access to Olympic National Park. A paved road twists and turns 17 miles up a steep 7 percent grade to the mile-high summit, where, on a clear day, you can gape at the breathtaking 360-degree views of mountain, valley, and sea. A lodge at the crest provides food and drink, and a concession offers ski and snowshoe rentals on winter weekends. Trails lead down into the backcountry, where you're likely to spot marmots, deer, and bald eagles—and if you're lucky, maybe an elk or a mountain lion. From Hurricane Ridge, thrill-seeking drivers and mountain bikers may get a kick out of Obstruction Point Road, a twisting gravel road that continues (without guardrails!) for another eight miles along the crest from the parking lot. In winter, the snowed-in road becomes a popular cross-country skiing trail.

Apart from the area right around Hurricane Ridge, most of the Olympic National Park backcountry is fairly wet and rugged. If you plan to camp overnight, be prepared, and be sure to get a permit from the Olympic National Park **visitors center** (360/565-3130) in Port Angeles, just south of US-101 on the road up to Hurricane Ridge. This is also the best place to pick up general information on the rest of the park, which extends all the way west to the rainforest areas along the coastal valleys.

Lake Crescent

One of the most idyllic spots in the entire Pacific Northwest, the fjord-like **Lake Crescent,** over 8 miles long and some 625 feet deep, lies right alongside two-lane US-101, just 18 miles west of Port Angeles. The placid surface reflects the clouds and surrounding peaks, including 4,537-foot Mount Storm King. To appreciate the tranquil beauty, rent a rowboat from the Lake Crescent Lodge and float around under your own steam. Starting from the lodge, a popular mile-long hike follows a well-maintained nature trail up to the delicate cascade of 90-foot **Marymere Falls,** while along the north shore an abandoned railroad grade is open to hikers and mountain bikers.

Incomparably situated along US-101 on the lake's southeast shore, **Lake Crescent Lodge** (360/928-3211, open May-Jan. only, except for the Roosevelt Fireplace Cottages open on the weekends, $156 and up) was originally built in 1916 and has been hosting visitors ever since. Fairly rustic rooms are available in the old lodge, which also has a cozy dining room. Other accommodations are available in the adjacent cabins and motel, though the whole place is booked solid on summer weekends, so reserve as soon as you can. Another nice place to stay is the **Log Cabin Resort** (360/928-3325 or 866/574-2708, camping from $25, rooms $125 and up), three miles north of US-101 on the "sunny northeast shore," with lodge rooms and waterfront A-frame cabins.

In the forested hills above US-101, **Sol Duc Hot Springs Resort** (866/476-5382, $170 and up) has family-friendly cabins and a restaurant set around a swimming pool and natural hot spring (around $13 for non-guests).

Hwy-112: Strait of Juan de Fuca

The **Strait of Juan de Fuca,** the narrow inlet that links the open Pacific with Puget Sound and divides the United States from Canada, was named for the Greek sailor (real name: Apostolos Valerianos) who first mapped it while working for the Spanish Crown in 1592. On a clear day, you can get some great views across the strait from Hwy-112, which runs along the shore from US-101 all the way to the tip of the Olympic Peninsula at Neah Bay. Though it looks like a great drive on the map, Hwy-112 is a very narrow and winding road with some surprisingly steep hills and thick woods that block much of the view, all of which (in addition to the plentiful logging trucks) can make it less than ideal for bicycling or even a scenic drive.

Neah Bay and Cape Flattery

From the crossroads at **Sappho** on US-101, Hwy-113 leads north, linking up with Hwy-112 on a long and winding 40-mile detour through Clallam Bay to **Cape Flattery,** the northwesternmost tip of the continental United States. The highway is paved as far as the town of **Neah Bay** (pop. 865), a tiny and somewhat be-

Along Hwy-112, you may pass a pair of fish-headed, human-legged, sneaker-wearing statues. Don't be alarmed.

draggled community that's the center of the Makah Indian Reservation. Salmon and halibut fishing, both by Makah and by visitors, is about the only activity here, though the tribe does have the impressive and modern **Makah Museum** (360/645-2711, daily, $5), one of the best anthropological museums in the state. Most of the displays are of artifacts uncovered in 1970, when a winter storm exposed the pristine remains of a 500-year-old coastal village that had been buried in a mudslide—the Pompeii of the Pacific Northwest. Other galleries display finely crafted baskets, a full-scale longhouse complete with recorded chants, and a whaling canoe from which fearless Makah harpooners would jump into the surf and sew up the jaws of dying whales, to keep them from sinking. If you want a special souvenir, the museum gift shop displays and sells a variety of high-quality arts and crafts made by Makah people.

The Hwy-112/113 route twists along the rocky and wooded shore of the Strait of Juan de Fuca, but reaching the actual cape itself isn't difficult. From Neah Bay, the well-maintained western half of the Cape Loop Road winds along the Pacific to a parking area that gives access to a trail that brings you to the top of a cliff overlooking the crashing surf and offshore

Cape Flattery

Tatoosh Island. On a sunny day it's a gorgeous vista, but if the weather's less than perfect (which it often is), your time would be much better spent inside the Makah Museum.

Forks

Bending southwest along the banks of the Sol Duc River, US-101 passes through miles of green forests under ever-gray skies to reach **Forks** (pop. 3,532), the commercial center of the northwestern Olympic Peninsula. Named for its location astride the Sol Duc and Bogachiel Rivers, Forks is a die-hard lumber town grappling with the inevitable change to more ecologically sustainable alternatives, mainly tourism. Visitors come to fish for steelhead during the late-summer runs, to beachcomb along the rugged coast, or to visit the remarkable rainforests of Olympic National Park. Today, the main attractions are related to the wildly popular teenage vampire novels and films of *The Twilight Saga,* which were set here in Forks (the movies were filmed elsewhere). You can also visit the quirky, summer-only **Forks Timber Museum** (360/374-9663, daily), on US-101 on the south edge of town, packed with handsaws, chainsaws, and other logging gear as well as antique cooking stoves and displays telling the town's history. There's also a forest-fire lookout tower perched outside the upper floor gallery.

With three gas stations and five motels, Forks is not a metropolis by any stretch of the imagination, but it does offer the best range of services between Port Angeles and Aberdeen. **Sully's Drive-In** (220 N. Forks Ave.) is a good burger stand on US-101 at the north end of town. There are also a couple of Chinese and Mexican places, plus pretty good pies at **Pacific Pizza** (870 S. Forks Ave.). Stay at **The Forks Motel** (351 S. Forks Ave., 360/374-6243, $60-160) or a more peaceful B&B, the **Miller Tree Inn Bed and Breakfast** (654 E. Division St., 360/374-6806, $120 and up), about half a mile east of US-101.

South of Forks along US-101, **Bogachiel State Park** (360/374-6356, around $20 for tents, $30 for RV hookups) has over 100 forested acres of very nice campsites (with showers!) along the Bogachiel River. Sites are first-come, first-served.

In the late 1990s, as part of an effort to preserve tribal traditions and instill pride in younger Makah, the Makah tribe resumed small-scale hunting of migratory gray whales, which they had voluntarily ceased when the whales became endangered a century ago. Though the hunting was largely ceremonial, the news raised the hackles of wildlife organizations, which filed lawsuits and staged loud protests to prevent whales from being killed.

For more information, contact the Forks **visitors center** (360/374-2531), next to the Timber Museum, which also serves as clearinghouse for *Twilight*-related tourism.

Hoh Rain Forest

Hoh Rain Forest

If you have time to visit only one of the lush rain forest areas of Washington's northwest coast, head for the **Hoh Rain Forest,** 12 miles south of Forks and then 18 miles east along a well-signed and well-paved road. Not only is this the most easily accessible of these incredibly lush, old-growth areas, the Hoh Rain Forest is also among the least disturbed, with a thick, wet blanket of vibrant green ferns, mosses, and lichens covering every inch of the earth at the foot of massive hemlocks, cedars, and towering Sitka spruce. Displays in-

side the visitors center tell all about the forest's flora and fauna and how they are affected by the massive rainfall here—upwards of 140 inches every year. There's also a wheelchair-accessible nature trail and a wide range of hiking trails, including the quickest access to the icy summit of 7,965-foot Mt. Olympus, 22 miles away in the glacier-packed alpine highlands at the heart of the park.

The closest services to the Hoh Rain Forest are in Forks, but budget travelers may want to take advantage of the $10-a-night bunks at the amiable **Rain Forest Hostel** (360/374-2270), 23 miles south of Forks along US-101 (between mile-markers 169 and 170), midway between the Hoh Rain Forest and the coast at Ruby Beach.

Kalaloch and the Pacific Beaches

Looping around the northern Olympic Peninsula, US-101 finally reaches the coast 27 miles south of Forks at **Ruby Beach,** where wave-sculpted sea stacks frame a photogenic, driftwood-strewn cove. From Ruby Beach, US-101 runs south through the wild coastal section of Olympic National Park, which is almost always foggy and cool, even when the weather's sunny and hot just a mile inland. While almost the entire coast south from Cape Flattery is protected within the national park, this is the only easily accessible stretch. Parking areas along the highway, numbered from Beach 6 to Beach 1 north to south, give access to 20 miles of generally deserted beach, backed by rocky bluffs and packed with tide pools, driftwood castles, and an incredible variety of flotsam and jetsam.

If you're very lucky, you might spy one of the rare Roosevelt elk, whose protection was one of the reasons Olympic National Park was established; if you're unlucky, you might come face-to-face with a mountain lion, which can be dangerous but generally avoids contact with humans.

At the southern end of this short but sweet stretch of coastline, between Beach 2 and Beach 3, 25 miles north of Lake Quinault,

Ruby Beach

Kalaloch Lodge (866/662-9928, $119 and up) is a modern resort, with a coffee shop and a nice restaurant overlooking a picturesque cove. There's also a gas station, a summer-only **ranger station** across US-101, and an oceanside **campground** just to the north.

Lake Quinault

Spreading in a broad valley at the southwest corner of Olympic National Park, **Lake Quinault** offers lush rain forest groves within a short walk or drive of most creature comforts. The lake has served for decades as a popular resort destination—cabins, lodges, and stores dating from the 1920s line the southern shore, just outside the park boundary. The old-growth forests here have survived intact, though the naked tracts of clear-cut timber along US-101 north and south of the lake give a good sense of what the area might have looked like had Teddy Roosevelt and friends not stepped in to protect it around the turn of the 20th century.

From US-101 at **Hoquiam,** Hwy-109 runs west and north along the Pacific Ocean through a series of small fishing ports and beach resorts to the heavily logged lands of the Quinault Indian Reservation.

Before or after the hike, stop at the **USFS ranger station** (360/288-2525) on the south shore, where you can get details of the other excellent hikes in the Lake Quinault area and pick up a map of the guided driving tour around the lake, including the location of the many record-size trees. The roughly four-mile-long **Quinault Loop Trail** winds on a path from the ranger station along crashing Cascade Creek up through an old-growth rain forest of alders and bigleaf maples, whose leaves grow upwards of 12 inches across (and provide some splendid "fall color"). Midway along, the trail crosses a raised wooden boardwalk through a fecund cedar swamp, then drops down again along another creek before returning by way of the lakeshore.

On the lakeshore right next to the ranger station, historic **Lake Quinault Lodge** (360/288-2900, $149 and up) is well worth a look, with a rustic but spacious lobby opening onto lakefront lawns, though the rooms could do with some TLC. The **Rain Forest Resort Village** (360/288-2535, $115 and up), at the east end of the lake, besides offering comfortable and reasonably priced accommodations (from camping to cabins) and very good food in the Salmon House Restaurant, also holds the **World's Largest Spruce Tree,** a 191-foot giant.

Grays Harbor: Hoquiam and Aberdeen

The Olympic Peninsula is cut off from the southern Washington coast by the spade-shaped bay of **Grays Harbor,** named for an early American sea captain and explorer, Robert Gray. Long the state's prime lumber port, Grays Harbor still processes huge piles of trees, but in many ways what's most interesting is the contrast between the two towns here, Hoquiam and Aberdeen.

At the western end of Grays Harbor, tidy **Hoquiam** (pop. 8,726; kind of rhymes with "requiem") celebrates its lumber-based history with an annual Loggers PlayDay bash, complete with ax-throwing and tree-climbing competitions, in early September. The rest of the year, get a feel for the bygone days of the lumber industry at the grand old timber-magnate mansion now housing **The Polson Museum** (1611 Riverside

The *Lady Washington* is a replica of one of the first American ships to explore the West Coast.

Ave., 360/533-5862, Wed.-Sun., $4), on US-101. Not surprisingly, it's devoted to local history, with information on logging.

East of Hoquiam along the Chehalis River at the head of Grays Harbor, **Aberdeen** (pop. 16,896) is much more heavily industrialized and thus has been even harder hit by the continuing downturn in the Northwest timber industry. Grunge-rock hero and Nirvana lead singer Kurt Cobain grew up in and around Aberdeen, which is why the city limits signs says "Come As You Are." There's also a couch Cobain may have slept on, and a decidedly odd statue of Cobain, in Aberdeen's **history museum** (113 E. 3rd St.). Ace road-trip photographer Lee Friedlander is from Aberdeen, too. The downtown area has more than a few rough edges, but it also holds one of the more high-profile of the state-sponsored efforts to move from timber to tourism: **Grays Harbor Historical Seaport Authority** (360/532-8611, daily, $3 donation), a mile south of Hwy-12. A reconstruction of one of American explorer Capt. Robert Gray's ships, the **Lady Washington,** can be toured—when she's not off on one of her regular "goodwill" cruises. The original ship was the first American vessel to visit the area, way back in 1788, and the replica was completed here in 1989 to celebrate the Washington State centennial.

Hwy-105: Westport and Tokeland

Between Hoquiam and Raymond, US-101 cuts inland from the coast, while an alternative route, Hwy-105, loops to the west past miles of cranberry bogs (and occasional wild elk) through the salmon-fishing town of **Westport.** Once called "The Salmon Capital of the World," and still a prime place for watching migrating gray whales, Westport is a very busy port—and one of Washington's few good surfing, clam-digging, and surf-kayaking beaches. The whole place really comes to life during the Labor Day seafood festival, but any time of the year the best stop is **Brady's Oysters** (360/268-0077), at the foot of the Hwy-105 bridge from Aberdeen, where you can buy fresh-shucked bi-valves by the half-gallon.

At the south edge of the peninsula, absorb more coastal character at the **Tokeland Hotel** (360/267-7006, $55-65), off Hwy-105 on the north shore of Willapa Bay, a truly historic landmark that has been welcoming visitors since the 1880s. Expect old-fashioned lodgings (shared bathrooms), a cozy family-style dining room serving classic dishes (pot roast with mashed potatoes, and suchlike), and unforgettable ambience.

Willapa Bay: Raymond and South Bend

One of the country's prime oystering grounds, **Willapa Bay** is sheltered from the Pacific by the Long Beach Peninsula and fed by the Nasalle, Willapa, and North Fall Rivers. There are very few towns or even villages on this stretch of US-101, which winds past tidal marshes, cattle ranches, and extensively clear-cut forests—which billboards proclaim to be "America's first industrial tree farm," giving dates of harvest, planting, and re-harvest, on a roughly 40-year cycle.

If the weather's right for a picnic, fresh shellfish can be had at bargain prices—live in the shell, or pre-shucked by the half gallon—from the area's many producers, wholesalers, and roadside stands. Look for them all along US-101 and up the Long Beach Peninsula.

At the northeast corner of Willapa Bay, on the south bank of the Willapa River, stand two towns that jointly embody the natural resource-based history and economy of the Pacific Northwest: **Raymond** (pop. 2,882) has the lumber mills, while **South Bend** (pop. 1,637) calls itself the "Oyster Capital of the World." South Bend's other claim to fame is its landmark **Pacific County Courthouse** (Mon.-Fri.), which since 1910 has loomed like a mini Taj Mahal on a hill just east of US-101. Step inside for a look at the 30-foot stained-glass dome above the rotunda, and wander through the lushly landscaped park next door.

If you want to stretch your legs, Raymond and South Bend are linked by the very nice **Willapa Hills Trail,** a walking and cycling path that follows an old railroad right-of-way along the Willapa River, amidst some engaging roadside metal sculptures of people canoeing, bird-watching, cycling, fishing, and generally enjoying the great outdoors.

Long Beach Peninsula

On the western side of Willapa Bay, the **Long Beach Peninsula** stretches for 28 miles of hard-packed sandy beaches along the roiling Pacific Ocean. Away from the few small towns, beaches and breakers abound along here, and you won't have any problem finding peace and solitude. The center of activity on the Long Beach Peninsula is the town of **Long Beach,** two miles from US-101, with a wanderable collection of crafts galleries and souvenir shops. A short walk west from "downtown" Long Beach, a wooden boardwalk winds along the coastal dunes, leading to a very rare sight: the reconstructed skeleton of a gray whale. Lewis and Clark saw similar bones when they passed by 200-plus years ago, and a **Discovery Trail** linking Corps of Discovery locations runs from here south to Ilwaco, near the mouth of the Columbia River.

"World's Largest Frying Pan"

If you can bear to stretch your budget a little, Long Beach is home to one of the coast's best B&Bs, historic **The Shelburne Inn** (4415 Pacific Way, 360/642-2442, $139 and up), located in the Seaview neighborhood (Pacific Way is also known as Hwy-103, the main road). The Shelburne Inn also houses a friendly pub. Long Beach is also the home of the nearly-10-feet-in-diameter **"World's Largest Frying Pan,"** which sits on a rack across from

Two statues sculpted by chain saws, in a small state park three miles west of the US-101 bridge across the Columbia River, mark the site where Lewis and Clark camped in December 1805 before heading south in search of better weather—which is about the only thing they never found on their epic trip.

the one-of-a-kind **Marsh's Free Museum** (409 S. Pacific Ave., 360/642-2188), a totally tacky (and wonderfully kitsch) collection of postcards, peep shows, and old-time arcade games.

The rest of the slender Long Beach Peninsula is quite quiet, dotted with cranberry bogs and historic fishing and oystering towns. In **Nahcotta,** a dozen miles north of Long Beach, you can stay overnight at the cozy **Moby Dick Hotel, Restaurant and Oyster Farm** (25814 Sandridge Rd., 360/665-4543, $90-150), where they grow, harvest, and serve their own bivalve treats. Just north, **Oysterville** is the peninsula's oldest community, with some nifty historic homes dating back to the 1850s. The peninsula comes to an end in the north at **Leadbetter Point State Park,** a great place for watching gulls, hawks, eagles, and migratory seabirds passing through on the Pacific Flyway.

Cape Disappointment

The high headland marking the place where the Columbia River finally merges into the Pacific Ocean, **Cape Disappointment** was named by the early explorer Capt. John Meares, who in 1788 incorrectly interpreted the treacherous sandbars offshore to mean that, despite reports to the contrary, there was neither a major river nor any mythical Northwest Passage here.

Besides the grand view of the raging ocean, the best reason to visit the cape is to tour the small but worthwhile **Lewis and Clark Interpretive Center** (360/642-3029, daily, $5), incongruously built atop a World War II-era artillery emplacement a short walk from the end of the road. On November 7, 1805, after five months and more than 4,000 miles, the explorers finally laid eyes on the Pacific from this point, and then they sat through nine days of continuous rain before fleeing south to Oregon. Displays inside the museum give the overall context for their journey of discovery, walking you through the different stages of their two-year round-trip. The small **"Cape D" lighthouse** stands atop a cliff, a half-mile walk from the Lewis and Clark museum, which is 200 feet above the Pacific Ocean. The more impressively photogenic **North Head Lighthouse,** on the ocean side of the peninsula a mile north of the museum, is the oldest on the West Coast.

The entire 1,882-acre area around the cape, including miles of beaches backed by rugged cliffs, is protected from development within **Cape Disappointment State Park** (360/642-3029), which has hiking, camping, and overnight lodgings in historic quarters next to North Head Lighthouse.

In recent years there have been a number of developments building on the area's Lewis and Clark connections, including the eight-mile Discovery Trail, which heads north to the town of Long Beach, and a series of thought-provoking installations by architect Maya Lin (creator of the Washington, D.C., Vietnam Veterans Memorial). Called the **Confluence Project,** and located mostly along the riverfront east of the museum, these works all deal with the coming together of the natural and man-made worlds, as well as the interaction of explorers and Native Americans. The installations range from boardwalks and interpretive trails (lined in places by quotations from Lewis and Clark's diaries) to a sculptural basalt "fish-cleaning" table.

The nearest services to Cape Disappointment—gas stations and a couple of cafés—are two miles away, back on US-101 in the rough-and-tumble fishing port of **Ilwaco,** where you can also enjoy the sophisticated yet simple and fresh seafood prepared at **Pelican Restaurant** (177 Howerton Way SE, 360/642-4034), on the harbor.

Southeast of Ilwaco, toward the Oregon border, US-101 winds along the north bank of the Columbia River, giving good views of the mighty river's five-mile-wide mouth.

OREGON

Rarely losing sight of the Pacific Ocean during its 340-mile jaunt along the Oregon coast, US-101 winds past rock-bound coast, ancient forests, and innumerable towns and villages. While the region also has its share of strip towns and places where the timber boom went bust, the beach loops, historic restorations, and more state parks per mile than any place in the country soften its few hard edges. Every 20 miles or so, you'll pass through attractive, if moderately touristy, towns populated by at most a few thousand people. As a general rule, it's the mileage between these hamlets that explains why most people visit: to take in one of the most dramatic meetings of rock and tide in the world.

Starting in the north along the Columbia River at historic

Astoria, one of the oldest settlements in the western United States, the route winds along the ocean past the very different beachfront hamlets of **Seaside** and **Cannon Beach** before edging slightly inland through the rich dairy lands of **Tillamook County.** Midway along, the popular vacation spots of **Lincoln City, Newport,** and **Florence** form the most developed corridor along the coast, but it's still easy to reach unpeopled stretches, especially at the remarkable **Oregon Dunes** stretching to the south. The dunes end abruptly at the heavily industrial port of **Coos Bay,** beyond which the natural beauty returns with a string of state parks and the diverse coastal towns of **Bandon, Port Orford, Gold Beach,** and **Brookings.**

Astoria

The oldest American city west of the Rockies, **Astoria** (pop. 9,477) is an upbeat mix of lovingly preserved past and busy contemporary commerce. Houses perched atop high hills overlook the Columbia River, creating a favorite backdrop for Hollywood movies. Despite its picturesque appearance, Astoria supports an active commercial fishing fleet, and dozens of tugboats guide tankers and container ships across the treacherous sandbars. Founded by and named after fur-trade magnate John Jacob Astor in 1811, Astoria protected the tenuous American claim to the Pacific Coast until the opening of the Oregon Trail brought substantial settlement. By the turn of the 20th century, Astoria was still Oregon's second-largest city, but the downturn in both salmon

Much as Forks, Washington, has benefited from its connections with the *Twilight* books and films, Astoria gets a boost in tourism numbers thanks to its starring role in the 1980s Steven Spielberg teen adventure film *The Goonies.*

fishing and logging since the end of World War II has caused an economic decline that, as always, town officials look to tourism to overcome.

US-101 crosses the Columbia River on the toll-free, high-level Astoria-Megler Bridge, completed in 1966, which drops you at the west end of the downtown waterfront. To get a sense of the lay of the land, follow the signs along 16th Street up Coxcomb Hill to the **Astoria Column** (daily dawn-dusk, $1 per car) for a view of the Columbia meeting the ocean, the coastal plain south to Tillamook Head, and the snowcapped Cascade Range (including, on a clear day, Mt. St. Helens) on the eastern horizon. A mosaic chronicling local history is wrapped like a ribbon around the column, tracing the many significant events in the town's past. A spiral staircase climbs to the top.

Back downtown **Flavel House Museum** (441 8th St., daily, $6) is a Queen Anne-style Victorian showplace restored as an elegantly furnished museum of Astoria's first millionaire, Columbia River pilot George Flavel. A half mile east, near the foot of 17th Street on the north side of waterfront Marine Drive, the **Columbia River Maritime Museum** (503/325-2323, daily, $12) displays a large and very impressive collection that tells the story of the lifeblood of this community: the Columbia River.

Fortify yourself at one of the many good seafood places along the water, starting at the funky, ever-popular **Columbian Café** (1114 Marine Dr., 503/325-2233, breakfast and lunch Sun.-Wed., breakfast, lunch, and dinner Thurs.-Sat.), where for over 30 years chef Uriah Hulsey has been preparing all sorts of fresh, veggie-friendly food in an impossibly cramped galley kitchen. Inspired by the chef's youthful immersion in the Cajun-Creole traditions of Louisiana, meals are massive yet reasonably priced, so be sure to arrive with an appetite. The café has been so popular, they've expanded next door with a **Voodoo Room** cocktail bar and pizza joint, which spills over into the restored

To find out about local issues and current events on the northern Oregon coast, pick up a copy of the excellent Daily Astorian newspaper, or tune to commercial-free **KMUN 91.9 FM** for NPR news and diverse programming.

1940s movie house next door. There's no better place to get a feel for Astoria, which once promoted itself through the slogan "We Ain't Quaint."

Another Astoria eating option is the casual **Ship Inn** (503/325-0033), serving halibut fish-and-chips under the bridge at Marine Drive and 2nd Street. Foodies might want to visit adjacent **Josephson's Smokehouse** (106 Marine Dr., 503/325-2190) to sample the delicious array of smoked salmon and Native American-style salmon "jerky," which is prepared on the premises and sold all over the country. One last option for excellent fish 'n' chips is the **Bowpicker** (503/791-2942), where chunks of fresh beer-battered albacore tuna and more is served up in an old fishing boat moored on the corner of 17th and Duane Street, a block south of the Maritime Museum. Seating is outdoors at picnic tables, so they close during windy and wet weather (and when they sell out of fish!).

To absorb a full portion of Astoria's addictive ambience, stay the night at the riverview **Crest Motel** (5366 Leif Erickson Dr., 503/325-3141, $65.50 and up), three miles east of town along US-30, or in town at the luxurious and historic **Hotel Elliott** (357 12th St., 503/325-2222, $129 and up). Astoria also has a handful of nice B&Bs, like the 1890s **Astoria Inn Bed and Breakfast** (3391 Irving Ave., 503/325-8153, $80 and up).

Fort Clatsop

In the conifer forests six miles south of Astoria and three miles east of US-101, and part of the extensive Lewis and Clark National Historical Park, the **Fort Clatsop National Memorial** (503/861-2471, ext. 214, daily, $3 per person during winter, $5 per person during summer) is a credible reconstruction of the encampment Lewis and Clark and company constructed during the winter of 1805-1806. Now the centerpiece of the sprawling, multi-state Lewis and Clark National Historical Park, Fort Clatsop has been fully (and in many ways more accurately) rebuilt after a 2005 fire destroyed the first (circa-1955) replica. The fort itself is joined by a range of exhibits in the visitors center. A longer (13-mile round-trip) trail leads to the coast. Summertime costumed rangers help conjure the travails of two centuries ago. The expedition spent three miserable months here, mingling occasionally

Fort Stevens, off US-101 on the way to Fort Clatsop, was the only continental U.S. fortification bombed during World War II, sustaining a shelling from a Japanese submarine on June 21, 1942.

with the native Clatsop and Chinook tribes but mostly growing moldy in the incessant rain and damp while being bitten by fleas, sewing new moccasins, and making salt in preparation for the return journey across the continent.

Gearhart

In between burly Astoria and the boisterous beach resort of Seaside, but a world away from its neighbors in terms of character and ambience, the tiny town of **Gearhart** (pop. 1,462) was the summer vacation home of influential chef and cookbook author James Beard. Beard's culinary legacy lives on in the **Pacific Way Bakery & Cafe** (601 Pacific Way, 503/738-0245), a half mile west of US-101, which offers the coast's best coffees and croissants, along with four-star lunches and dinners. Like many places along the Oregon coast, it's closed Tuesday and Wednesday.

Seaside

Nothing along the Oregon coast prepares you for the carnival ambience of downtown **Seaside** (pop. 6,457), one of Oregon's oldest seafront resorts. Ben Holladay, who built a resort here in the 1870s, included a racetrack, zoo, and plush hotel to lure Portlanders to ride his rail line to the beach. Come during spring break, or on a weekend during July or August, and join the 50,000 or more visitors wandering among the saltwater-taffy stands and video-game arcades along Broadway, or cruising the concrete boardwalk (called The Prom) along the beach.

Where Broadway meets the beach, a small traffic circle known locally as The Turnaround is marked by a statue and a sign proclaiming the town "The End of the Lewis and Clark Trail." South of here, between Beach Drive and The Prom, is a replica of the Lewis and Clark salt cairn, where the explorers boiled seawater nonstop for seven weeks to produce enough salt to preserve meat for their return trip east. From the south end of Seaside, you

statue of explorers Lewis and Clark at the end of the trail in Seaside

centennial commemorative stamp

Portland

Portland, Oregon's largest city, is located inland from the coast near the confluence of the Willamette and Columbia Rivers. Due to its strategic location, the pioneer municipality grew so fast it was nicknamed Stumptown for the hun-

dreds of fir stumps left by early loggers, and while railroad tracks and other heavy industrial remnants are still highly visible around town, Portland's riverfront park and numerous winding greenways show that this mini metropolis is not a smokestack town but a community that values art and nature as highly as commerce. Along with the largest (5,000-acre Forest Park) and the smallest (24-inches-in-diameter Mill Ends Park) urban parks in the nation, and one of the coolest urban skate parks anywhere (under the Burnside Bridge), Portland also has more movie theaters, restaurants, microbreweries, and bookstores per capita than any other U.S. city.

The oldest part of Portland has, over the past few years, been renovated into a lively Old Town district, where cast-iron facades of 120-year-old buildings hold some of the city's most popular bars, clubs, and cafés. (Not to mention general weirdness magnets like the 24-Hour Church of Elvis, most recently found at 408 N.W. Couch Street.) South of Old Town along the river, an ugly freeway has been torn down to form the mile-long Tom McCall Waterfront Park, and west of the river, downtown Portland centers on lively Pioneer Courthouse Square, at 6th Avenue and Yamhill Street. South of the square, the South Park Blocks between Park and Ninth Avenues were set aside as parklands in the original city plan and are now bounded by Portland's prime museums. One essential Portland place is north of the square: **Powell's Books** (503/228-0540), at 1005 W. Burnside Street across from the Blitz-Weinhard Brewery, is the largest (and certainly among the best) new-and-used bookshop in the world.

One of the largest and oldest ballparks in the minor leagues, the circa-1926 Civic Stadium, downtown off Burnside at 1844 SW Morrison, has been fully renovated and redubbed PGE Park, home to the **Portland Beavers** (503/553-5555), the San Diego Padres' top farm club.

Along the river south of town, **Oaks Park** (503/233-5777) is a wonderful circa-1905 amusement park, with ancient and modern thrill rides all packed together in a sylvan, oak tree–dotted park.

PRACTICALITIES

Air travelers can land at Portland International Airport (PDX), but most long-distance flights here come and go via Seattle's Sea-Tac, which is only about 2.5 hours' drive north, via the I-5 freeway. Getting around public-spirited Portland is a breeze thanks to the combination of an efficient bus system and a light rail train (called MAX; 503/238-7433).

Though it doesn't have a trendy reputation, Portland does have some great restaurants in all stripes and sizes. **Esparza's Tex-Mex,** 2725 SE Ankeny Street (503/234-7909), hidden away behind a hole-in-the-wall facade a block south of E. Burnside Street, is worth searching out for its smoky pork tacos and a jukebox featuring Tejano, norteño, and Marty Robbins hits. For more traditional Portland fare, head to **Jake's Famous Crawfish** (503/226-1419), at 401 SW 12th Street, which for over a century has been the place to go for the finest, freshest seafood. For meat, nothing beats the **Ringside** (503/223-1513), near PGE Park at 2165 W. Burnside Street, long famous for its great beef, fine fried chicken, monster Walla Walla sweet onion rings, and Hemingway-esque ambience. If your taste happens to run more to Marilyn Manson than Marilyn Monroe, you'll probably prefer to eat across town at **Dots Cafe** (503/235-0203), at 2521 SE Clinton Street, a late-night hangout that has comfy dark booths, great black-bean burritos, microbrews, and pool tables.

There are all sorts of places to stay in Portland, starting with a pair of popular **HI-Portland Hostels,** one east of downtown at 3031 Hawthorne Boulevard (503/236-3380) and a newer one in the Northwest District, at 425 NW 18th Avenue (503/241-2783). The stylish, comfortable,

Powell's City of Books

and close-to-downtown **Hotel DeLuxe** ($150 and up; 503/219-2094) is a newly renovated boutique hotel at 729 SW 15th Avenue. If you feel like splurging, try another impeccably restored downtown landmark, the **Heathman Hotel** ($199 and up; 503/241-4100 or 800/551-0011), at 1009 SW Broadway, with an elegant lobby and sumptuously appointed (if somewhat small) rooms.

The best source of visitor information on Portland is the **Portland Visitors Association** (503/275-9750 or 800/962-3700), on Pioneer Courthouse Square.

can follow a challenging but very rewarding five-mile trail over Tillamook Head to Ecola State Park.

A half mile north of downtown, housed in a wood-shingled old motor court on the banks of the Necanicum River, the **Seaside International Hostel** (930 N. Holladay Dr., 503/738-7911) has dorm beds, private rooms, canoes and kayaks, an espresso bar, and nightly movies. There are dozens of motels and a handful of B&Bs in Seaside, booked solid in summer and serene, verging on lonely, come wintertime. The best breakfasts are served up on Broadway just west of US-101 at the **Firehouse Grill** (841 Broadway, 503/717-5502). For fish 'n' chips, head to the south edge of town along US-101, where the no-frills **Bell Buoy** (503/738-6348) has daily fresh halibut and excellent crab cocktails, best eaten on the outdoor deck overlooking the Necanicum River. There are also pizza places and ice cream stands all over Seaside.

Ecola State Park

Just north of Cannon Beach, a mile south of the junction between US-101 and US-26 from Portland, the rain-forested access road through **Ecola State Park** (503/436-2844, day use only, $5 per car) leads you to one of the most photographed views on the coast: Looking south you can see Haystack Rock and Cannon Beach with Neahkahnie Mountain looming above them. Out to sea, the sight of **Tillamook Rock Lighthouse** to the northwest is also striking. Operational from 1881 to 1957, the lighthouse is now used as a repository for the ashes of people who've been cremated.

The rest of Ecola State Park protects a series of rugged headlands stretching for nine miles along the coast, with many forested hiking trails, including some of the most scenic portions of the Oregon Coast Trail system. The park also marks the southernmost extent of Lewis and Clark's cross-country expedition. Clark and a few other members of the Corps of Discovery expedition traversed the area in search of supplements to their diet of hardtack and dried salmon. The word *"ecola"* means whale in the Chinookan tongue and was affixed to this region by the Lewis and Clark expedition, who found one of these leviathans washed up on a beach. They happily bought 300 pounds of tangy whale blubber from local Indians, but these days you'd better bring your own lunch to picnic atop bluffs with sweeping views of the rock-strewn Pacific. The view from the top of **Tillamook Head,** which rises 1,200 feet above the sea at the heart of the park, was memorialized by explorer William Clark as "the grandest and most pleasing prospect" he had ever beheld.

Cannon Beach

Unlike many Oregon coast towns, **Cannon Beach** (pop. 1,690) is hidden from the highway, but it's one place you won't want to miss. Though it's little more than a stone's throw south of boisterous Seaside, Cannon Beach has long been known as an artists' colony, and while it has grown considerably in recent years thanks to its popularity as a weekend escape from Portland, it retains a peaceful, rustic atmosphere.

Every summer, Cannon Beach hosts one of the largest and most enjoyable **sand castle competitions** on the West Coast, with some 10,000 spectators and as many as 1,000 participants turning out with their buckets and spades. In terms of traditional tourist attractions, there's not a lot to do, but Cannon Beach is an unbeatable place in which to stop and unwind, or to take long walks along the nine-mile strand and then retreat indoors to the many good galleries, cafés, and restaurants. For breakfast or brunch, fill up on eggs Benedict at **The Lazy Susan Cafe** (126 N. Hemlock St., 503/436-2816, closed Tues.); it also serves a stupendous array of ice cream at its "scoop shop" up the street. Another great, casual gourmet place to eat is **Ecola Seafoods** (208 N. Spruce St., 503/436-9130), a market and restaurant selling and serving locally caught fish and shellfish—including tempura-battered Chinook salmon, grilled halibut, smoked mussels, and an excellent $5 chowder.

Reasonably priced rooms near the beach and town can be found at the oceanfront **Sea Sprite at Haystack Rock** (280 S. Nebesna St., 503/436-2266, $99 and up).

Cannon Beach

South of Cannon Beach, the beach loop runs along a spectacular grouping of volcanic basalt plugs, notably 235-foot-high **Haystack Rock.** Elsewhere along the Oregon coast, there are at least two more geological outcrops called Haystack Rock, a bigger one off Cape Kiwanda and another down near Bandon.

Neahkahnie Mountain and Oswald West State Park

South of Cannon Beach, US-101 rises high above the Pacific. Nowhere else along the Oregon coast does the roadbed offer such a sweeping ocean view. Soaring another thousand feet above the highway is **Neahkahnie Mountain,** which offers unsurpassed views up and down the coast. About 10 miles south of Cannon Beach at **Oswald West State Park** (800/551-6949), a half-mile trail winds beneath the highway through an ancient forest to driftwood-laden (and surfer-friendly) **Short Sands Beach** and the tide pools of **Smuggler's Cove.** Named for an early governor of Oregon who successfully proposed preserving and protecting the beaches of Oregon as state (rather than private) property, Oswald West State Park is a good start for longer hikes, to weather-beaten Cape Falcon or across US-101 to the summit of Neahkahnie Mountain.

South of Neahkahnie Mountain, and thus spared much of the stormy coastal weather (annual rainfall hereabouts averages more than 80 inches), is the upscale resort town of **Manzanita.** Nearby **Nehalem Bay State Park** (503/368-5154) has a large campground with hundreds of sites and plenty of hot showers. US-101 continues through a series of small towns before winding inland past the sloughs and dairy country along Tillamook Bay.

Tillamook

Tillamook (pop. 4,400), where cows outnumber people, sprawls over lush grasslands at the southern end of Tillamook Bay. Its motto, "Land of cheese, trees, and ocean breeze," conjures a clear sense of a place where

Tillamook Cheese Factory

the high school football team is cheered on by shouts of "Go Cheesemakers!" Tillamook (a Salish word meaning "land of many waters") is dominated by the **Tillamook Cheese Factory** at the north end of town, one of the busiest tourist draws in the state. Inside, a self-guided tour with informational placards traces

Tillamook cheese-making from the last century to the present, and a glassed-in observation area lets you watch the stuff being made and packaged.

Tillamook's other attraction is east of US-101 and south of town. One of the world's largest wooden structures—296 feet wide, 1,072 feet long, and nearly 200 feet tall, enclosing more than seven acres of open-span floor space—has been preserved as the **Tillamook Air Museum** (503/842-1130, daily, $12 adults). Built in 1942, the structure is now a museum telling the story of the World War II surveillance blimps kept here by the U.S. Navy. There are also displays about other dirigible craft (like the ill-fated *Hindenburg*) as well as a world-class collection of vintage airplanes (from MiG fighters to an elegant, twin-tailed P-38 Lightning), plus a theater and a restaurant, all making for a fascinating and unusual stop. The building used to be one of a pair of hangars, but the other one burned down in 1992.

Three Capes Loop

US-101 veers inland for 50 miles between Tillamook and Lincoln City, the next sizable town south. If time and weather are on your side, head west along the coast via the well-signed, 40-mile-long **Three Capes Scenic Route.** Running northwest from Tillamook, the loop reaches the mouth of Tillamook Bay at **Cape Meares,** which has a restored 1890 lighthouse and an oddly contorted Sitka spruce known as the Octopus Tree.

Heading south through the coastal villages of **Oceanside** and **Netarts,** the loop proceeds through dairy country until it climbs onto the shoulder of **Cape Lookout,** where a small sign proclaiming Wildlife Viewing Area marks the beginning of a 2.5-mile trail that leads through an ancient forest to the tip of the cape, 100-plus feet above the water. Besides the coastal panorama, in winter and spring this is a prime place to view passing gray whales. From the trailhead, the middle path leads to the cape, while others to the left and right lead down to the water. **Cape Lookout State Park** (503/842-4981) has the area's most popular campground, where tent sites, yurts, and cabins come with hot showers and other creature comforts.

The Oregon coast's most famous promontory, **Cape Kiwanda,** sees some of the state's wildest surf battering the

Seven miles south of Tillamook, a turnoff east follows a bumpy, one-mile access road leading to the highest waterfall in Oregon's Coast Range, 319-foot **Munson Creek Falls.** From the parking area at the end of the road, a short trail leads to this year-round cascade.

sandstone headland. Across from the cape is yet another **Haystack Rock,** this one being a 327-foot-tall sea stack, a half mile offshore. Along the beach south of the cape, surfers ride waves while fisherfolk skid their small dories along the sands most afternoons—a sight worth hanging around to see.

The southernmost settlement on this scenic alternative to US-101 is neighboring **Pacific City.**

Lincoln City

The most developed section of the Oregon coast stretches for miles along US-101 through **Lincoln City** (pop. 7,930), seven miles of strip malls, outlet stores, fast-food franchises, and motels. With more than 1,000 oceanside rooms, Lincoln City does offer some of the coast's cheapest lodging, especially in the off-season when sign after sign advertises rooms for as low as $35 a night. Along with inexpensive accommodations, Lincoln City has some great places to eat. After a day on the beach or in the forests, tuck into some four-star fish tacos, chowders, or battered seafood at **J's Fish & Chips** (1800 SE US-101, 541/994-4445).

One more unforgettable culinary attraction hereabouts sits five miles northeast of Lincoln City, just east of US-101 on Hwy-18, the main road to and from Portland: the **Otis Café** (1259 Salmon River Hwy., 541/994-2813, daily breakfast, lunch, and dinner), which immortalizes American road food, offering excellent waffles and other breakfast treats along with epicurean lunches and fresh berry pies for dessert.

South of Lincoln City, **Siletz Bay** is a bird-watcher's paradise, where hawks and herons and thousands of other seabirds (along with chinook salmon and cutthroat trout) are protected within a federal wildlife refuge.

South of Lincoln City, 2.5 miles east of US-101, the **Drift Creek Covered Bridge** is the oldest of some 50 such structures in the state.

Depoe Bay was originally known as **Depot Bay,** named after a local Siletz Indian who worked at the local U.S. Army depot and called himself Charlie Depot.

Depoe Bay

Depoe Bay has an appeal, but so much of its natural beauty is obscured from the highway by gift shops or intruded upon by traffic that you've got to know where to look. In his book *Blue Highways,* William Least Heat-Moon wrote "Depoe Bay used to be a picturesque fishing village; now it was just picturesque." While it's true that most of the commercial fishing is long gone, you can still park your car along the highway and walk out on the bridge to watch sportfishing boats move through the narrow channel in and out of what the *Guinness Book of Records* rates as the world's smallest navigable natural harbor.

The **Sea Hag** restaurant (541/765-2734), on US-101 in downtown Depoe Bay, is a time-tested breakfast place—run by the same people for more than 40 years! Be sure to time your trip so you can enjoy Betty Taunton's fresh-baked pies at the equally legendary **Spouting Horn** (541/765-2261), overlooking the harbor. For a place to stay, try the very popular **Inn at Arch Rock** (70 NW Sunset St., 800/767-1835, $99 and up).

Cape Foulweather and the Devil's Punchbowl

Between Depoe Bay and Newport, the roadside scenery along US-101 and the parallel "old road," now signed as the Otter Crest Loop, is dominated by miles of broad beaches and sandstone bluffs, including the 500-foot headland of **Cape Foulweather,** named by Capt. James Cook and offering a 360-degree coastal panorama. The Otter Crest Loop has frequently been closed by slides and reconstruction efforts, but you can reach it from many access roads. With fine old bridges and numerous vistas, it's a great drive—or bicycle route.

Farther south, midway between Depoe Bay and Newport, the aptly named **Devils Punchbowl** gives a ringside seat on a frothy confrontation between rock and tide. In the parking area you'll find a small lunch café. Other than its famous clam chowder, claim to fame of this branch of Newport's **Mo's** remains a visit from Bruce Springsteen on June 11, 1987.

Newport

Another old fishing community turned tourist nexus, **Newport** (pop. 9,989) became popular in the 1860s on the strength of sweet-tasting Yaquina Bay oysters, which were in demand from San Francisco to New York City and are still available at local restaurants. Oysters, crabs, and clams, along with sea otters, sea lions, sharks, and seabirds, are the stars of the show at the large and modern **Oregon Coast Aquarium** (541/867-3474, daily, $19.95 adults), south of Newport across the Yaquina Bay Bridge. The aquarium includes an aquatic aviary, where tufted puffins and other shorebirds cavort in a simulated rockbound coastal habitat, and over 40,000 square feet of similarly ecofriendly exhibits, many of them outdoors.

On the north side of the US-101 bridge over Yaquina Bay, turn onto Hurbert Street and head for the bayfront, where boatyards and fish-packing plants service a working harbor. Though it's still one of the state's largest fishing

The coast and inland forests along the Siletz River near Depoe Bay and Newport were the primary location of the Ken Kesey novels and films *One Flew Over the Cuckoo's Nest* and *Sometimes a Great Notion*.

The old-growth forests of the **Drift Creek Wilderness** east of Waldport are prime nesting areas for the endangered northern spotted owl, whose numbers are still declining.

inside the aquarium tunnel at the Oregon Coast Aquarium

ports, much of Newport's bayfront has been consumed by souvenir shops, a wax museum, a Ripley's Believe It or Not, and other tourist traps. But you'll also find the original **Mo's** (622 SW Bay Blvd., 541/265-2979), a locally famous seafood restaurant.

North of the harbor is **Nye Beach,** an interesting mélange of old-fashioned beach houses and destination resorts on the western side of US-101. Nye Beach is home to hotels, motels, and the bohemian **Sylvia Beach Hotel** (267 NW Cliff St., 541/265-5428, $115 and up), *the* place to stay in Newport for anyone of literary bent. All rates include breakfast. Sumptuous dinners are available, too.

Waldport

If you want to avoid lines and general tourist bustle, **Waldport** is a nice alternative to the resort towns surrounding it. Tourism is low-key here, and you can still sense the vestiges of the resource-based economy, a by-product of the town's proximity to rich timber stands and superlative fishing. Stop along US-101 at the **Alsea Bay Historic Interpretive Center** (541/563-2133) for interesting exhibits on coastal transportation and the local Alsea tribe, as well as a telescope trained on waterfowl and seals in the bay. The center sits at the southwest foot of the modern span that, in 1991, replaced the historic (circa-1936) art deco-style bridge.

Four miles south of Waldport, halfway to Yachats, **Beachside State Recreation Site** (541/563-3220) has a very popular campground, with hot showers, RV hookups, and a lovely stretch of sandy beach. They have **yurts** ($45 a night), too.

Yachats

On the way into **Yachats** (pop. 690; pronounced "YA-hots"), beach loops on either side of the Yachats River give a sense of why the area is called "the gem of the Oregon coast." It's a great place to wander and get lost and found again, especially at the beautiful Ocean Road State Natural Site, where incredible views along a one-mile loop road look out over crashing waves, tide pools, blowholes, and, in winter, gray whales migrating offshore.

Yachats

Back in town, for the past 30-plus years, **Leroy's Blue Whale** (580 Hwy-101 N., 541/547-3399), on US-101, has been serving breakfast, lunch, and dinner every day, featuring fluffy pancakes, fresh chowders, and fine fish-and-chips. Perhaps because of its connections to Portland, Yachats also has some excellent coffee places, including a nameless espresso stand along US-101 on the south side of town, next to the "Devil's Churn" rock formation where the rising tide crashes through a coastal chasm.

The word "cottage" is a popular lodging label around Yachats, usually referring to a moderately priced, self-contained cabin or duplex with a kitchen. On US-101 there are a half dozen different cottage complexes, each fronting the beach. Among the many attractive, comfortable, and affordable options is **Beachcomber Cottages** (95500 S. US-101, 541/547-3432, $80).

Cape Perpetua

For more than 300 miles along the Oregon coast, US-101 abounds with national forests, state parks, and viewpoints. But unless you have your whole lifetime to spend here, **Cape Perpetua,** two miles south of Yachats, deserves most of your attention. Stop first at the **Cape Perpetua Visitor Center** (541/547-3289), just east of US-101, for seacoast views and exhibits on forestry and area history. From the visitors center, trails lead across the highway past wind-bent trees, piles of seashells and other artifacts left behind by native peoples, excellent tide pools, and two coastal rock formations: the **Devil's Churn,** right on US-101 at the north edge of Cape Perpetua, and the **Spouting Horn,** off US-101 a half mile south of the visitor center. During stormy seas, especially in winter, both are amazing spectacles, with the Spouting Horn shooting huge spouts of foam 50 feet high into the air through a hole in the roof of a collapsed, underwater lava cave.

You can reach the top of 800-foot-high Cape Perpetua itself by following a two-mile-long road, marked by Cape Perpetua Viewpoint signs and leaving US-101 100 yards or so north of the visitors center. Once atop the cape, walk the **Whispering Spruce Trail,** a half-mile loop around the rim of the promontory that yields, on a clear day, 150-mile views of the Oregon coast from a rustic, WPA-built stone observation point.

The friendly folks at the visitors center can also point you toward Cape Perpetua's very attractive campground. Or if you want a more comfortable place to spend the night, the **Oregon House** (541/547-3329, $95 and up), on US-101 six miles south of Cape Perpetua, has spacious apartment-like rooms, some with fireplaces and ocean views, and all with access to the well-tended grounds and trails leading down the bluffs to a gem of a sandy cove.

Heceta Head and the Sea Lion Caves

Halfway between Cape Perpetua and Florence, a small bridge just south of Carl G. Washburne Memorial State Park marks the turn-off to **Heceta Head Lighthouse,** perhaps the most photographed beacon in the United States. Built in 1894, it was named for the Spanish mariner who is credited with being the first European to set foot in the region. You'll have to be content with gazing at it across the cove from a small but rarely crowded beach, unless you stay at the quaint old lighthouse keeper's quarters, restored as an unforgettable **B&B** (541/547-3696, $234 and up).

A half mile south of Heceta Head Lighthouse, 11 miles north of Florence, traffic along US-101 slows to a stop at the gift shop that serves as the entrance to **Sea Lion Caves** (daily, $15 adults). You can ride an elevator down to the world's largest sea cave, the only mainland rookery for the Steller sea lion. Fall and winter offer the best times to see (and smell!) these animals, which throng together here during mating season. When the weather is nice, you can often watch them swimming in the ocean (for free, without the seal smells . . .) from a viewpoint 100 yards up US-101.

Florence

If first and last impressions are enduring, **Florence** is truly blessed. As you enter the city from the north, US-101 climbs high above the ocean; coming from the south, travelers are greeted by the graceful **Siuslaw**

SIUSLAW RIVER BRIDGE, FLORENCE

LOOKING TOWARD TEN MILE LAKE AND SUTTON LAKE

River Bridge, perhaps the most impressive of a handful of WPA-built spans designed by Conde McCullough and decorated with his trademark Egyptian obelisks and art deco stylings. Unfortunately, first impressions feel a little misleading, since much of what you can see from US-101 is a bland highway sprawl of motels, gas stations, and franchised restaurants.

The best part of Florence, **Old Town,** is just upstream from that landmark bridge, along the north bank of the Siuslaw River. Here, among Bay Street's three blocks of interesting boutiques and galleries, you'll find a number of cafés and seafood restaurants, like **Bridgewater Fish House** (1297 Bay St., 541/997-1133, closed

Tues.). Old Town Florence is also home to the very welcoming **Edwin K Bed and Breakfast** (1155 Bay St., 541/997-8360, $135-200), a lovely white Craftsman-style home built in 1914 by one of the town's founders.

"Dune Country"

For nearly 50 miles south of Florence, US-101 has an extensive panorama of oceanfront dunes. Though the dunes are often obscured from view by forests, roadside signs indicate access roads to numerous dunescapes on both sides of the highway. Coming from the north, the first of these access points is **Jessie M. Honeyman**

Fans of Frank Herbert's ecological sci-fi saga *Dune* may already know that the stories were inspired by the Oregon Dunes, south of Florence.

Memorial State Park, three miles south of Florence, where rhododendrons line a trail leading to a 150-foot-high dune overlooking a mirage-like lake.

Giant rhododendrons and tumbledown shacks that rent out dune buggies and ATVs line US-101 between Florence and Coos Bay. Dune buggy tours ranging from peaceful to exhilarating are offered by **Sandland Adventures** (541/997-8087), less than a mile south of Florence's Siuslaw River Bridge.

Before setting out on any extended exploration, your first stop should be the USFS-run **Oregon Dunes National Recreation Area Visitors Center** (541/271-6000) at the junction of US-101 and Hwy-38 in **Reedsport,** along the Umpqua River midway between Florence and Coos Bay at the heart of the dunes. The helpful rangers can provide detailed information on hiking and camping throughout the park. Reedsport itself has a line of motels and burger joints—**Don's Main Street Family Restaurant** (2115 Winchester Ave., 541/271-2032), on US-101, has legions of fans for its hearty, inexpensive food and excellent home-made pies.

Perhaps the best introduction to the bewildering geography of the dunes region is **Umpqua Dunes,** nine miles south of the Reedsport visitors center. Another popular walk starts from **Eel Creek Campground,** heading for just under three miles across small marshes and conifer groves en route to the sea, negotiating lunar-like dunes soaring 300-500 feet—some of the tallest in the world. Another nice trek leaves from **Tahkenitch Lake,** a popular largemouth bass fishing spot north of Gardiner, and gives a more in-depth look at the dunes' diverse flora and fauna, including swans and (very rarely!) black bears.

Coos Bay

Even if you race right through, it's quite apparent that **Coos Bay** (pop. 15,967), once the world's largest lumber port, retains a core of heavy industry. Many of the big mills have closed, and one has been replaced by **The Mill Casino,** a resort complex operated by native Coquille Indian tribe. You can still watch huge piles of wood chips, the harbor's number-one export, being loaded onto factory ships in the harbor east of US-101. The chips are sent to Asia, where they're turned into paper.

There's very good seafood and other meals available at **Sharkbites Cafe** (240 S. Broadway, 541/269-7475), on southbound US-101. Microbrews and a wide range of beer-friendly German dishes are served at the **Blue Heron Bistro** (100 Commercial Ave., 541/267-3933), across from the visitors bureau. There's no shortage of easy-to-find lodging, including **Motel 6** (1445 N. Bayshore Dr., 541/267-7171, $50 and up) on US-101.

Behind the Coos Bay visitors bureau, a monument remembers the region's favorite son, middle- and long-distance runner Steve Prefontaine, who electrified the athletic world before his death in a 1975 car wreck, at the age of 24. An annual 10K memorial run is held in September.

Nine miles west of Coos Bay, in the busy commercial and sport-fishing port of **Charleston,** you'll be welcomed to town by an unlikely sight: a flipper-waving statue of 1960s-era advertising icon Charlie the Tuna (of StarKist seafood fame).

Shore Acres State Park

The historical antecedents for Coos Bay port development were laid a century ago by the Simpson Lumber Company, whose ships transported Oregon logs around the world. The ships returned with exotic seeds that were planted in the Simpson estate's garden, 12 miles west of Coos Bay via the Cape Arago Highway. Though the Simpson house burned to the ground in 1921, the five acres of formal gardens are still a floral fantasia, now open to the public as **Shore Acres State Park** (daily 8am-dusk). Besides the formal gardens, which are illuminated during the Christmas holiday season, there's an observation tower above wave-battered bluffs and a trail down to a delightful beach.

On the way to Shore Acres from Coos Bay is **Sunset Bay State Park,** perhaps Oregon's best swimming beach. South of Shore

Acres is **Cape Arago State Park,** complete with tide pools and seals (and seal pups in springtime) lounging on offshore rocks. Mostly level trails lead along the coastline from Shore Acres to Sunset Bay and Cape Arago State Parks. If you're tempted to stay overnight and explore the lovely region, consider taking advantage of one of Oregon's best-kept secrets: the roomy, tent-like **yurts** (800/452-5687, $40) available for overnight rental at Sunset Bay and in a dozen other state park beauty spots.

Bandon

There's no sharper contrast on the Oregon coast than the difference between industrial Coos Bay and earthy **Bandon** (pop. 3,066), 24 miles to the south. Here, in the **Old Town** section along the banks of the Coquille River, are several blocks of galleries, crafts shops, and fine restaurants, marked by a gateway arch off US-101. Start a tour of Old Town at the corner of 1st and Baltimore, where Big Wheel General Store houses the **Bandon Driftwood Museum** (daily, free), which gives a good sense of Bandon's back-to-the-land, hippie ethos. A more academic introduction to the town and region can be had at the **Bandon Historical Society Museum** (270 Fillmore Ave., 541/347-2164, Mon.-Sat., daily in summer, $2 adults), in the old City Hall along US-101. Its exhibits on area history, cranberries, and local color are artfully done, and the building is easy to find, so be sure to stop. South of town, Beach Loop Drive runs along a ridge overlooking a fantastic assemblage of coastal monoliths.

For fish-and-chips along the waterfront, the **Bandon Fish Market** (249 1st St. SE, 541/347-4282) is cheap, cheerful, and very very good; a block to the east, looking more like a tackle shop than a restaurant, **Tony's Crab Shack** (541/347-2875) is another local landmark, famous for fish tacos, chowders, and silky crab sandwiches.

Outside of town, the exclusive and expensive (but open to the public) **Bandon Dunes Golf Resort** (541/347-4380 or 888/345-

6008, $75-250 per golf round for resort guests) has been drawing raves from golfers, well-heeled vacationers, and landscape architects alike. Designed to preserve and enhance the "natural" scenery in the style of Scottish "links"

courses rather than the anodyne green swaths that characterize most suburban country club courses, Bandon Dunes offers golf, deluxe accommodations, and a nice restaurant.

South of Bandon, 9.5 miles north of Port Orford, **Cape Blanco** is considered—by Oregonians, at least—the westernmost point of land in the contiguous United States. Named by early Spanish explorers for the white shells encrusting the 245-foot cliff face, the cape is also the site of Oregon's oldest (circa

Bandon Beach

1870) and highest lighthouse. Set back from the cliffs in forested woodlands, **Cape Blanco State Park** (541/332-2973) has hot showers and a few cabins ($42), along with a spacious campground ($22). The headland offers great views of the rugged coastline plus a good chance of seeing gray whales spouting and leaping offshore.

Port Orford and Humbug Mountain

Pastoral sheep ranches, cranberry bogs, berry fields, and Christmas tree farms dominate the 25-mile stretch south of Bandon, but as you pull into **Port Orford** (pop. 1,133), you can't help but notice a huge volcanic plug abutting the crescent-shaped shoreline. Known as **Battle Rock,** in memory of a battle (re-enacted every 4th of July) in which early settlers fought off a party of hostile Indians, the rock is impressive from the harbor below, while a trail climbs up to the windblown summit. Due to the southwest orientation, which subjects the harbor to turbulent winds and constant waves, fishing boats have to be lowered into the water by crane, but surfers (and kite-surfers and windsurfers) don't seem to mind.

Six miles south of Port Orford you'll come to **Humbug Mountain State Park,** whose 1,756-foot elevation flanks the west side of the highway. It's one of the coast's highest peaks, rising directly off the beach. Its steep contours and tree-covered slopes are best appreciated from

People who keep track of these things say that tiny Port Orford is the "most westerly incorporated city in the continental United States." Others grant it the less-welcome title of "rainiest place on the Oregon coast."

the steep but well-maintained three-mile trail that climbs to the summit. The mountain's name may have been bestowed by prospectors who found that tales of gold deposits here were just "humbug"—but the views from the top are splendid.

Prehistoric Gardens

On the west side of the highway, midway between Port Orford and Gold Beach, you'll come across one of the Oregon coast's tackiest but most enduring and enjoyable tourist traps, the **Prehistoric Gardens** (541/332-4463, daily, $12 adults). Standing out like a sore thumb on this otherwise unspoiled stretch of US-101, brightly colored, more or less life-sized dinosaur sculptures inhabit the evocatively lush green forest. Since 1953, when amateur paleontologist E. V. Nelson sculpted his first concrete *T. rex,* nearly two dozen more have been added to the forest menagerie.

Gold Beach

Gold Beach was named for the nuggets mined from the area's black sands during the mid-19th century. Despite its name, this is one coastal town where the action is definitely *away* from the beach. The **Rogue River** defines the northern city limits and is the town's economic raison d'être. During salmon season, Gold Beach hotels and restaurants fill up with anglers, while **jet-boat tours** of the wild river are also a draw. **Jerry's Rogue Jets** (541/247-4571 or 800/451-3645, $55 and up adults), by the bridge at the north end of town, takes passengers upstream to the isolated hamlet of **Agness,** where a homespun **mountain lodge** (meals around $15) serves family-style fried-chicken lunches and dinners. Other trips head farther upstream to the Rogue River rapids and the roadless wilderness areas of the **Siskiyou National Forest.**

The usual motel rooms are available along US-101, but for a more memorable visit, try the **Tu Tu' Tun Lodge** (96550 North Bank Rogue, 541/247-6664 or 800/864-6357, $160 and up). Set on a hill above the Rogue River, seven miles upstream from the coast, this upscale fishing lodge (pronounced "ta-TWO-tun") has plushly rustic rooms and a great restaurant.

Samuel H. Boardman State Scenic Corridor

Between Gold Beach and Brookings, US-101's windy, hilly roadbed is studded with the cliffside ocean vistas, giant conifers, and boomerang-shaped offshore rock formations of **Samuel H. Boardman State Scenic Corridor.** The park covers 12 of the "Fabulous 50" miles between the two towns, and all of the features come together at

Natural Bridges Cove. Located just north of the **Thomas Creek Bridge** (the highest bridge in Oregon), this turnout is easy to miss despite being well signed because, from the highway, it appears to be simply a parking lot fronting some trees. From the south end of the parking lot, however, a short trail through an old-growth forest leads to a viewpoint several hundred feet above three natural rock archways standing out from an azure cove.

Brookings: Harris Beach State Park

The drive through the malled-over main drag of **Brookings** offers only fleeting glimpses of the Pacific, and if you're hoping for a first or last "Wow!" before or after the 300-plus other miles of coastal Oregon's scenic splendor, these few miles along the California border may be somewhat anticlimactic. That said, Brookings does have beautiful **Azalea Park** (which is gorgeous during the April-June spring bloom). The popular, welcoming beachfront B&B rooms at **Lowden's Beachfront Bed & Breakfast** (14626 Wollam Rd., 541/469-7045, $109 and up), just west of US-101, offer direct access to a driftwood-strewn beach.

Just north of Brookings, one final piece of Oregon's abundant natural beauty has been preserved at **Harris Beach State Park,** across US-101 from the Oregon Welcome Center. Here you can walk down to a driftwood-laden beach and look out at Bird Island, where tufted puffins and other rare birds breed.

Heading south, just over the California border from Brookings lies Redwood National Park, truly one of the West Coast's great places.

Southern Oregon's coastal forests yield the increasingly rare and disease-threatened Port Orford cedar, a very valuable (up to $50,000 per tree) and very fragrant wood popular for use in Japanese home construction.

Mt. Emily, just east of Brookings, was bombed by a submarine-launched Japanese seaplane in September 1942. Though the Japanese plans to ignite the entire coastline in a massive forest fire fizzled, the attack weakened a short-lived secession movement by southern Oregonians and northern Californians to establish a new state called Jefferson.

CALIFORNIA

Stretching along the Pacific Ocean for roughly a thousand miles from top to tail, the
California coast includes virgin wilderness,
the cutting edge of cosmopolitan culture,
and the full spectrum in between. For almost the entire way, coastal roads give quick and easy access to
the best parts, with panoramic views appearing so
often you'll simply give up trying to capture it all.

Starting in the north, the green forests of the
Pacific Northwest continue well beyond the state border, forming a mountainous seaside landscape that lasts
until the edge of metropolitan **San Francisco.** Along this stretch you'll
find a number of old logging and fishing towns, varying from the
burly blue-collar likes of **Eureka** and **Crescent City** to the upscale ambience of **Mendocino,** in and amongst endless acres of redwood forest.

At the approximate midpoint of the California coast sits **San
Francisco,** deservedly ranked among the world's favorite cities. The
100 miles of coast stretching south from San Francisco hold numerous remnants of the Spanish and Mexican eras, exemplified by the
town of **Monterey** and the beautiful mission at **Carmel.** Beyond here
is another stretch of wild coastline, the rugged country of **Big Sur.**

Beyond the southern edge of Big Sur, opulent **Hearst Castle**
marks the start of what most people consider Southern
California, the rivers and trees of the north giving way to golden
beaches, grassy bluffs, and considerably denser populations. A
pair of very pleasant small cities, Midwestern-feeling **San Luis
Obispo** and ritzy **Santa Barbara,** make excellent stops in themselves, smoothing the transition into the environs of **Los
Angeles,** the unwieldy megalopolis that, seen from the I-5 freeway that links Los Angeles and **San Diego,** seems like one mon-
strous, 100-mile-long suburb. While it's true that the natural
beauty that brought so many people to Southern California in the
first place is increasingly endangered, some lovely, almost untouched places remain, hidden away but within easy access of the
fast lane. We've pointed them out; enjoy them while they last.

Jedediah Smith Redwoods State Park

The northernmost of the great redwood groves, **Jedediah Smith
Redwoods State Park** covers nearly 10,000 acres of virgin forest
along the banks of the Smith River. Stretching east of US-101, and
most easily accessible from US-199, the park offers over 20 miles

of usually uncrowded hiking trails through the pristine wilderness; it is considered by many the most perfect of all the redwood forests. One of the most enjoyable trails leads through **Stout Grove,** past tall trees and a number of summertime swimming holes along the Smith River.

There's also a good **campground** (800/444-7275) with hot showers. For fans of roadside kitsch, there's one unique spot along US-101 in the hamlet of **Smith River,** 15 miles north of Crescent City: **Ship Ashore** (707/487-3141), a gift shop, restaurant, campground, and motel along US-101, marked by a grounded but still handsome 1920s yacht, inside which is a gift shop.

The **Smith River** and **Jedediah Smith Redwoods State Park** were named in memory of the legendary mountain man Jedediah Strong Smith, who in 1826 at the age of 27 led the first party of Americans overland to California. Smith also blazed a trail over South Pass through the Rocky Mountains that was later used by the Oregon Trail pioneers.

Outside Crescent City, 3,000 of California's most violent criminals are kept behind bars, and often in solitary confinement, in the notorious Pelican Bay State Prison, which opened in 1989.

Crescent City

The county seat and only incorporated city in Del Norte County, **Crescent City** (pop. 7,394) is best treated as a base from which to explore the surrounding wilderness. The foggy weather that helps the redwoods thrive makes the city fairly depressing and gray, and what character it developed since its founding in the 1850s has been eroded by storms; a giant tsunami, caused by the 1964 earthquake off Alaska, destroyed much of the city. The more recent tsunami unleashed by the 2011 quake in Sendai, Japan, was less destructive but drowned one man and caused millions of dollars in damage to boats moored in the Crescent City harbor.

Crescent City includes the familiar lineup of motels and restaurants, plus local options like the **CC Diner and Ice Cream** (1319 Northcrest Dr., 707/465-5858), on the north side of downtown, a half mile west of US-101. For overnight, one only-in-California option is the **Curly Redwood Lodge** (701 S. Redwood Hwy./US-101 S., 707/464-2137, $60 and up), a nicely maintained 1950s motel made from a single, sawn-up redwood tree.

Del Norte Coast Redwoods State Park

Spreading south from the Jedediah Smith redwoods, **Del Norte Coast Redwoods State Park** runs along the Pacific Ocean (and US-101) for about eight miles, containing more than 6,000 acres of first- and second-growth redwoods as well as brilliant blooms of rhododendrons, azaleas, and spring wildflowers. Del Norte also protects miles of untouched coastline, the best stretch of which is accessible from the end of **Enderts Beach Road,** which cuts west from US-101 just north of the park entrance. From here, a 30-mile trail follows the coast to Prairie Creek. The state park area is bounded on the south by an undeveloped section of **Redwood National Park.**

Trees of Mystery and Klamath

Hard to miss along US-101, thanks to the massive statues of **Paul Bunyan** and **Babe the Blue Ox** looming over the highway, the **Trees of Mystery** (707/482-2251, daily, $15 adults) are literally and figuratively the biggest tourist draws on the Northern California coast. Along the Trail of Tall Tales, chainsaw-cut figures, backed by audiotaped stories, stand in tableaux at the foot of towering redwoods. There's also a SkyTrail gondola lifting passengers up into the treetop canopy, a huge gift shop, and an excellent, free museum of Native American art and artifacts. Across the highway, **Motel Trees** (707/482-3152, $75 and up) has standard rooms and a café.

Along the banks of the mighty Klamath River, four miles south of the Trees of Mystery, the town of **Klamath** (pop. 779) is a brief burst of highway sprawl, supported by anglers who flock here for the annual fall salmon runs—provided there are any fish left to catch. Fisherfolk, walkers, and kayakers all avail themselves of the enduringly popular **The Historic Requa Inn** (707/482-1425, $119 and up), a friendly, comfortable homestead run by members of the local Yurok Indian tribe right on the riverfront. At the south end of Klamath town, take a drive right through the **Tour Thru Tree** ($5), then cross the Klamath River on a bridge graced by a pair of gilded cement grizzly bears.

All the land along the Klamath River is part of the extensive **Hoopa Valley Indian Reservation,** which stretches for over 30 miles upstream from the Pacific Ocean.

Prairie Creek Redwoods State Park

The largest of the trio of north coast state redwood parks, **Prairie Creek Redwoods State Park** is best known for its large herd of endangered Roosevelt elk, which you can usually see grazing in the meadows along US-101 at the center of the park, next to the main **ranger station** (707/465-7347). A modern freeway carries US-101 traffic around, rather than through, the Prairie Creek redwoods. To reach the best sights, detour along the well-signed Newton B. Drury Scenic Parkway, which follows Prairie Creek along the old US-101 alignment through the heart of the park.

Another elk herd can be spotted among the coastal dunes at **Gold Bluffs Beach,** which stretches for 11 miles through untouched wilderness; there are trails leading from US-101, or you can follow Davison Road northwest from US-101, 3 miles south of the ranger station. Apart from the elk, Prairie Creek offers a basic campground in a beautiful setting: the usual mix of old-growth redwood trees, which here, more than in the other parks, mingle with dense growths of Sitka spruce and Douglas firs to form a near rain forest of greenery.

Redwood National Park

Established in 1968, and enlarged since then, **Redwood National Park** protects the last vestiges of the more than two million acres of primeval redwood forest that once covered the entire Northern California coastline. To be honest, alongside the gorgeous groves in the adjacent Smith, Del Norte, and Prairie Creek State Parks, the trees preserved here aren't by any means the oldest, largest, or most beautiful. In fact, much of the federal parkland is second- or third-growth timber, clear-cut as recently as

the 1960s. Though redwoods are the fastest-growing softwoods on earth—growing 3-5 feet a year when young—the groves here can look rather disappointing compared to those in nearby areas. But, they do serve a valuable role as an environmental buffer zone even if they're not exactly a tree-lover's pilgrimage site.

That said, Redwood National Park does hold two special sights, including the **Lady Bird Johnson Grove,** on Bald Hill Road two miles east of US-101, where the new park was dedicated in 1969.

The groves of giant trees in Redwood National Park were used as a location for the Star Wars film *Return of the Jedi,* in which the characters cruised through the forest on airborne cycles. Patrick's Point played a starring role in the sequel to *Jurassic Park.*

Ten miles farther up this road, and a long hike beyond that, the **Tall Trees Grove** (free permit required) holds one of the world's tallest trees, the 360-plus-foot Libbey Tree, whose trunk measures over 14 feet in diameter.

At the south end of the park, the roadside-strip town of **Orick** stretches toward the coast, where the main Redwood National Park **Thomas H. Kuchel Visitor Center** (707/465-7765) stands at the mouth of Redwood Creek.

Patrick's Point State Park

If your idea of heaven is sitting on a rocky headland listening to the roar of the Pacific while watching the sunset or looking for passing gray whales, you won't want to pass by **Patrick's Point State Park** (707/677-3570). Three different 200-foot-high promontories at the heart of the park provide panoramic views, while the surrounding acres hold cedar and spruce forests (no redwoods), open pastures bright with wildflowers, great tide pools, a wide dark-sand beach, and three **campgrounds** (800/444-7275) with hot showers. There's also the preserved and restored remnants of a Yurok village, a redwood dugout canoe, and a garden of traditional herbs.

Continuing south, US-101 becomes a four-lane freeway along the ocean to Arcata and Eureka, but most of the old US-101 alignment winds along the cliff tops between Patrick's Point and the small town of **Trinidad.** Along this road you'll find some places to stay, like the **Trinidad Inn** (1170 Patrick's Point Dr., 707/677-3349, $75 and up), about three miles south of the park entrance. A little farther down this old stretch of US-101 is **The Larrupin' Cafe** (1658 Patrick's Point Dr., 707/677-0230), which serves up bountiful portions of very fresh all-American food in a friendly, homey ambience—it's California cuisine without the snooty pretense you sometimes find farther south.

Arcata

The most attractive and enjoyable town on the far north coast of California, **Arcata** (pop. 15,700) makes the best first (or last, depending upon the direction you're traveling) overnight stop south of the Oregon border. The presence of Humboldt State University's campus on the hills above US-101 accounts for the town's youthful, nonconformist energy. Cafés, bookstores, bars, and crafts shops surround the lively **Arcata Plaza,** two blocks west of US-101 at 9th and G Streets, incongruously graced by palm trees and a statue of President McKinley. The *Utne Reader* once rated Arcata as the most enlightened town in California. Spending even a little time in this vibrant, cooperative Ecotopia may make you wonder whether or not you really do have to race back to the big-city, 9-to-5 grind.

You can admire the town's many elaborate Victorian-era cottages, hunt wild mushrooms, clamber over sand dunes, or hike in the redwoods; afterward, relax with a cup of tea or, better yet, a soak in a hot tub at homey **Cafe Mokka** (495 J St., 707/822-2228), the coast's only combo sauna and espresso bar. Just off the plaza, **Jambalaya Arcata** (915 H St., 707/822-4766) is a nightclub serving burgers, micro-brew beers, and (of course) jambalaya. More good

The author Bret Harte was run out of Arcata by angry townspeople in 1860, after writing an editorial in the local paper criticizing a massacre of a local Wiyot tribe.

PLEASE
DO NOT CLIMB
ON ROCKS

Inland from Arcata along scenic US-299, the town of **Willow Creek** claims to be the heart of Bigfoot Country, boasting a large statue of the furry beast to prove it. One of the state's most scenic drives (or bike rides), US-299 continues east over the coast range through the beautiful **Trinity Alps** to **Weaverville,** well-preserved site of a mid-1850s gold rush, before linking up with I-5 at Redding.

food, good beer, and good live music are on the menu at the very popular "HumBrews," a.k.a. the **Humboldt Brews** (856 10th St., 707/826-2739). For a complete selection of foodstuffs and supplies, and more insight into the local community, head to the large and stylish **North Coast Co-op** (811 I St.), a block north of the plaza.

For a place to stay, the centrally located **Hotel Arcata** (708 9th St., 707/826-0217 or 800/344-1221, $89 and up) is right on the plaza, or you can take your pick of the usual motels along US-101.

Eureka

Evolving into a lively artists' colony from its roots as a fairly gritty and industrial port, **Eureka** (pop. 28,606) was well known to fur trappers and traders long before it became a booming lumber and whaling port in the 1850s. Thanks to the lumber trade, Victorian Eureka grew prosperous, building elaborate homes, including the oft-photographed but closed to the public **Carson Mansion** along the waterfront at 2nd and M Streets, two blocks west of US-101.

One unique thing to see in Eureka is the **Romano Gabriel Sculpture Garden** (315 2nd St.), displayed in a plate-glass showcase. This brilliantly colorful folk-art extravaganza of faces and flowers originally stood in the front yard of local gardener Romano Gabriel, who made them out of discarded packing crates and other recycled materials over a period of some 30 years before his death in 1977.

Along with dozens of well-preserved Victorian houses, Eureka has done a fine job of finding new uses for its many ornate commercial buildings, most of which have been preserved to house art galleries, cafés, and restaurants in what's now called **Old Town,** a half dozen blocks between the waterfront and US-101. This historic downtown quarter has a huge number of good places to eat and drink, including **Ramone's Bakery & Cafe**

(209 E St., 707/445-2923) and the pub-like **Cafe Waterfront** (102 F St., 707/443-9190), serving excellent fish-and-chips, chowders, and other fresh seafood right on the harbor. And if that's not enough to sate your appetite, for yet more fish-and-chips and a pint or two of ale, head along to the **Lost Coast Brewery** (617 4th St., 707/445-4480).

Accommodation options range from roadside motels to upscale places like the **Carter House Inns** (301 L St., 707/444-8062, $189 and up), a re-created Victorian manor with spacious rooms and a big breakfast in the morning. For a more authentic Victorian experience, stay at one of California's most delightful B&Bs, **Abigail's Elegant Victorian Mansion** (1406 C St., 707/444-3144, $225 and up). A real treasure in a land of nice B&Bs, this magnificently restored 1888 Eastlake-style home has been opulently decorated with real antiques and Bradbury & Bradbury wallpapers by the hospitable Belgian-born innkeeper, Lily Vieyra and her husband Doug.

For further information, about Eureka or anywhere in the whole glorious Redwood Empire region, contact the **Humboldt County Convention and Visitors Bureau** (1034 2nd St., 707/443-5097 or 800/346-3482).

Samoa

Even if you're just passing through, don't miss the chance to visit the old mill town of **Samoa,** across the bay from Eureka but easily reachable via the Hwy-255 bridge. On a narrow peninsula between the bay and the open ocean, the unique **Samoa Cookhouse** (707/442-1659, daily breakfast, lunch, and dinner) was built in 1890 to feed the many hungry men living and working in the "company town" lumber mill here. The mill is long gone now, but the cookhouse remains in operation as a sort of living history center, packed with logging memorabilia and blue-collar character. So take a seat at one of the 20-foot-long

KINETIC GRAND CHAMPIONSHIP

Humboldt County's creative community comes alive every Memorial Day weekend for the world-famous **Kinetic Grand Championship,** in which participants pedal, paddle, and otherwise move themselves and their handmade vehicles across land and sea. Part art, part engineering, and part athletic competition, the Kinetic Grand Championship is like nothing you've seen before. Also known as the "Kinetic Sculpture Race" and "The Triathlon of the Art World," the event begins midday Saturday and runs until Monday afternoon, as a mind-boggling array of mobile contraptions make their way over land, sand, and sea from the town square of Arcata to the main street of Ferndale, twice crossing chilly Humboldt Bay. Past winners have included everything from dragons and floating flying saucers to Egyptian pyramids (named Queen of Denial) and a Cadillac Coupe de Ville.

"Just for the Halibut": racing along Samoa Peninsula

tables (redwood, of course, covered in checkered oilcloth), soak up the history, and dig into the family-style feasts (all-you-can-eat!). There are no menus, just huge platters of food at very reasonable prices.

Ferndale

Well worth the 10-mile round-trip detour west of US-101, the historic town of **Ferndale** (pop. 1,371) is an odd fish along the woodsy Northern California coast, a century-old dairy town that would look more at home in middle America. The three-block-long, franchise-free Main Street includes a fully stocked general store, the **Golden Gait Mercantile** (421 Main St.). Whitewashed farmhouses dot the pastoral valleys nearby. Ferndale's diverse history is well documented inside the **Ferndale Museum** (515 Shaw Ave., 707/786-4466, hours vary), where some of the wacky racers that take part in the annual **Kinetic Grand Championship** are displayed.

Ambling along Main Street is the best way to get a feel for

Rule Number One of the Kinetic Grand Championship is that all of the "sculptures" must be people-powered; beyond that, imagination is the primary guide. Many "rules" have developed over the years since the race was first run in 1969, including such pearls as: "In the Event of Sunshine, the Race Shall Proceed," but most of these emphasize the idea that maintaining style and a sense of humor are at least as important as finishing the fastest. Since the Grand Prizes are valued at somewhere around $14.98, racers take part solely for the glory.

Spectators are expected to be active participants, too, so be prepared to shout and scream and applaud the competitors, or even jog or bike or kayak alongside them. There are many great vantage points along the route, but you have to be in the right place on the right day. Before noon on Saturday there's a pre-race lineup around Arcata Plaza, from where racers head through the streets of Arcata out toward the Manila Dunes before spending the first night in downtown Eureka. Sunday morning the racers head across Humboldt Bay from Field's Landing, then camp out overnight on the beach. Monday's trials include another water crossing, and it all culminates in a mad dash down the Main Street of Ferndale, surrounded by cheering multitudes. It's all good fun, and a great focus for a visit to this remarkable corner of the world.

Ferndale, and if you build up an appetite, there are many good places to eat. One of the oldest cafés in the West, **Poppa Joe's** (409 Main St., 707/786-4180), serves great diner food in a no-frills Victorian-era storefront, while one of California's earliest hotels features a family-friendly Italian restaurant, **The Hotel Ivanhoe Restaurant & Saloon** (315 Main St., 707/786-9000, dinner only). On the main road midway between town and US-101 is another fast-foodie landmark: the **No Brand Burger Stand** (1400 Main St., 707/786-9474), where all the tasty patties are hand-formed from local grass-fed beef. Fab fries and luscious milk shakes, too. Yum.

Along with its good food options, Ferndale is equally well supplied with places to stay. Right off the heart of Main Street is the clean and tidy **Redwood Suites** (332 Ocean Ave., 707/786-5000, $125 and up). Also nice

The area around Ferndale has been hit by numerous earthquakes, including a destructive tremor in April 1992 that registered 7.2 on the Richter scale.

is **The Shaw House Inn** (703 Main St., 707/786-9958, $135 and up), an 1854 American Gothic masterpiece with B&B rooms for rent.

The Lost Coast

Between Ferndale and Rockport, the main US-101 highway heads inland along the Eel River. But if you have time and a taste for adventure, head west from Ferndale along the narrow, winding Mattole Road, which loops around Cape Mendocino through the northern reaches of the so-called **Lost Coast,** a 100-mile stretch of shoreline justly famous for its isolated beauty. By road, you can only get close to the ocean at a few points—the few miles south of Cape Mendocino, and again at the fishing resort of **Shelter Cove,** west of Garberville—but hikers can have a field day (or week) exploring the extensive coastal

wilderness. Some 50 miles of rugged, untouched coastline, packed with tide pools and driftwood-strewn beaches, have been preserved in a pair of parks, the **King Range National Conservation Area** in the north and the **Sinkyone Wilderness State Park** farther south.

Besides the Hwy-211/Mattole Road, which makes a 70-mile loop between Ferndale and the Rockefeller Forest section of Humboldt Redwoods State Park, a network of rougher and even more remote routes allows auto access to the Lost Coast, linking the hamlet of **Honeydew** with coastal Hwy-1 near Rockport. If you do explore this wild (and very rainy) region, take a good map and plenty of food and water, and be careful.

The Lost Coast area was the site of the first oil well in California, which was drilled in the 1860s in the town of **Petrolia,** but is now long gone.

For further information on the Lost Coast, contact the **Bureau of Land Management** (1695 Heindon Rd., 707/825-2300); its office is off US-101 on the north side of Arcata.

Scotia

Back along US-101, on the banks of the Eel River midway between the coast and the Humboldt Redwoods, **Scotia** was the last true company town left in California. The Pacific Lumber Company (a.k.a. PALCO) built it and, for most of the 20th century, owned and operated everything, from the two huge wood-cutting mills to the 10 blocks of pastel-painted houses, church, and schools that constituted this little community of about 1,000 people.

The lumber mills used to be the heart and soul of the town, as well as Scotia's main tourist attraction, but after a 1980s junkbond leveraged buyout and subsequent asset-stripping PALCO finally went bankrupt in 2007. Since then the town and the mills have struggled to find a way forward, but Scotia is still a proud and photogenic place, well worth a look and a wander.

In summer, the heart of Scotia is the rustic and historic **Winema Theater,** which screens movies on weekend nights (plus an old-fashioned Saturday matinee). The one place to stay in town is the rustic **Scotia Inn** (100 Main St., 707/764-5338, $75 and up), which has B&B rooms and a very good restaurant. Part of the old lumber mill has been reconfigured into a biofueled home for the excellent (and 100 percent organic) **Eel River Brewery,** which operates a popular tasting room and restaurant at its original location near Ferndale, off US-101 in the hamlet of Fortuna (1777 Alamar Way, 707/725-2739).

Humboldt Redwoods State Park

Sheltering the biggest and best collection of giant coastal redwoods anywhere in the world, **Humboldt Redwoods State Park** is an exceptionally breathtaking corner of an exceptionally beautiful region. Covering more than 53,000 acres along the Eel River, this is the true heart of redwood country, containing the largest and most pristine expanses of virgin forest as well as some of the largest, tallest, and most remarkable trees.

The protection of the mighty redwood forests of Northern California was made possible not by the state or federal governments but primarily by the efforts of the **Save the Redwoods League** (114 Sansome St., Suite 1200, San Francisco, CA 94104, 415/362-2352), a private organization that has raised, since its founding in 1918, millions of dollars to

Save The Redwoods
L E A G U E®

buy or preserve over 185,000 acres of redwood forest. To support these efforts, write or call the league.

Even if you're just passing through, be sure to turn onto the amazing **Avenue of the Giants,** 31 miles of old highway frontage between Pepperwood and Phillipsville. This sinuous old road snakes alongside, and sometimes under, the faster and busier US-101 freeway, which is carried on concrete stilts through the park. In and amongst the natural wonders along the Avenue of the Giants are a handful of man-made ones: The **Eternal Tree House** (free admission) in Redcrest, with a friendly and inexpensive café, and the **Shrine Drive Thru Tree** ($6), in Myers Flat, are just two of the many good-natured "tourist traps" in this neck of the woods. At the north end of the park you'll find an impressive collection of trees in the well-marked **Founder's Grove,** where a half-mile nature trail leads past the 362-foot-tall, possibly 2,000-year-old **Dyerville Giant,** lauded as one of the world's tallest trees before it fell during the winter of 1991.

Once you've done the Avenue of the Giants, if you want to escape the crowds and the freeway rumble, head west from Founder's Grove across US-101 to the 10,000-plus-acre **Rockefeller Forest.** This expansive grove is one of the largest old-growth forests in the world and includes two of the world's champion trees, each over 360 feet tall and some 17 feet in diameter.

The best source of information on the park is the **Visitor Center** (707/946-2263), midway along the Avenue of the Giants in Weott;

there's a pleasant state-run **campground** (800/444-7275) with showers right next door. You may have to drive a ways north (to Ferndale, Eureka, or Arcata) or south (to Garberville) from the park to find an exceptional meal, though there are a few nice places to stay, like the historic **Myers Country Inn** (707/943-3259, $200 and up), midway along the Avenue of the Giants in Myers Flat. Farther south, the hamlet of Miranda holds the pleasant **Miranda Gardens Resort** (766 Ave. of the Giants, 707/943-3011, $105 and up), with a handy general store and rustic cabins backing onto redwood groves.

Garberville and Redway

Apart from its recurring presence in the national media during the occasional high-profile raids on local "medical marijuana" plantations, the redwood country town of **Garberville** is a pretty quiet, peaceful place. The US-101 freeway bypasses the town, and locals walk and talk to each other along the half dozen blocks of Redwood Drive, the well-signed business loop off the highway.

> The Garberville/Redway area is home to a pretty unusual community of old hippies and off-the-grid libertarians, who share their music and politics on noncommercial local radio station **KMUD 91.1 FM.**

Enjoy an early-morning breakfast with the old-time locals at the **Eel River Cafe** (801 Redwood Dr., 707/923-3783), or an espresso and healthy food at the **Woodrose Café** (911 Redwood Dr., 707/923-3191), a block south. Garberville also has all the motels you could want, including the **Motel Garberville** (948 Redwood Dr., 707/923-2422, $50 and up).

Two miles west of Garberville on the old highway, **Redway** is worth the short side trip for an organic burger at **Deb's Great American Hamburgers** (707/923-2244), or a slice of pizza or fine dinner at **The Mateel Cafe** (707/923-2030), a health-conscious gourmet haunt at the center of town. The Reggae on the River festival, organized by the energetic **Mateel Community Center** (707/923-3368), attracts world-class performers and thousands of fans every July.

Along US-101, four miles south of Garberville, one of the region's most characterful places is the stately **Benbow Historic Inn** (707/923-2124, $99 and up), a circa-1926 mock Tudor hotel with a nice restaurant offering afternoon tea and scones on a sunny terrace overlooking Lake Benbow.

Leggett: The Chandelier Drive-Thru Tree

No longer even a proverbial wide spot in the road since the US-101 freeway was diverted around it, **Leggett** marks the southern end of the Humboldt redwoods. At the south end of "town," a mile from the US-101/Hwy-1 junction along the old highway, stands one of

AVENUE OF THE GIANTS

The stretch of historic US-101 through the redwood country of Humboldt County, frequently called the **"Avenue of the Giants,"** is lined by pristine groves of massive trees and provides boundless opportunities to come face-to-face with your own insignificance in nature's greater scheme of things. If you tire of this display of natural majesty, or simply want to keep it in context with the modern "civilized" world, you're in luck: Every few miles, amongst the stately trees, you'll come upon shameless souvenir stands selling redwood burl furniture and chainsaw sculptures, as well as wonderfully tacky tourist traps like the Legend of Bigfoot. Many of these hyper-tacky attractions now exist only in memory (and on old postcards!), but none of

at the end of Leggett, the "original" Drive-Thru Tree

the survivors is big or bold enough to detract from the main event—the big trees—and since they've been in operation since the early days of car-borne tourism, they're as much a part of the redwood experience as the trees themselves. Most charge only a few dollars' admission, so there's not a lot to lose.

While you're encouraged to stop at any and all of them—at least long enough to buy a postcard or two—the most tried-and-true attraction is the **Trees of Mystery,** marked by huge statues of Paul Bunyan and Babe the Blue Ox along US-101 in Klamath, well north of the official Avenue of the Giants. In Myers Flat is the **Shrine Drive-Thru Tree,** at 13078 Avenue of the Giants (old US-101), which wagon-borne travelers drove through more than a century ago. Two more classics are found in the south: One of the best stops in redwood country, **Confusion Hill** in Piercy is one of those places where water runs uphill and the rules of physics seem not to apply, and there's also a little railway train here that chugs uphill to a very nice grove of trees. Finally, at the **Chandelier Drive-Thru Tree,** in Leggett off old US-101 on Drive Thru Tree Road, drive your car through a 315-foot redwood tree, still growing strong despite the gaping hole in its belly.

the redwood region's most venerable and worthwhile roadside attractions, the "original" **Chandelier Drive-Thru Tree** (daily dawn-dusk, $5). In addition to the famous tree, which had the six-foot-nine-inch-tall tunnel cut through it in the 1930s, there's an above-average gift shop with a broad range of books, postcards, and schlocky souvenirs.

Nearby, the 16-acre grounds of **Big Bend Lodge** (707/925-2440, summer only, $149) has nine very quaint riverfront cabins, perfect for lazy days floating, swimming, or fishing. South of Leggett, US-101 runs inland racing toward San Francisco, while scenic Hwy-1 cuts west over the coastal mountains to Mendocino, winding slowly south along the Pacific.

Westport

From US-101 at Leggett, a very narrow stretch of Hwy-1 twists up and over the rugged coastal mountains before hugging the coast through the weatherbeaten logging and fishing community of **Westport.** The tiny town has more than you might expect, including a cozy 1970s motel and deli on the ocean side of Hwy-1, called the **Westport Inn** (707/964-5135, $70 and up), and the newer and more upscale **Westport Hotel** (707/964-3688) two blocks south, which has a sauna and (sometimes) a restaurant and welcoming pub with frequent live music. (But be warned: when the restaurant is closed it's a half-hour drive to the nearest places to eat, in Fort Bragg.) The small and informal **Howard Creek Ranch Inn** (707/964-6725, $90 and up) three miles north of Westport offers comfortable B&B rooms, an outdoor hot tub, and easy access to the driftwood-laden beach. (Like Westport Hotel, it's a half-hour drive to the nearest restaurants.) Farther south, **MacKerricher State Park** protects seven miles of rocky coast and waterfront pine forest. An old logging railroad right-of-way, called Ten-Mile Haul Road, has been brought back into use as a hiking and cycling path that covers most of the eight miles between the north end of MacKerricher and the town of Fort Bragg, crossing over Pudding Creek on a recently renovated railroad trestle. The park offers the chance to see harbor seals and migrating gray whales (in winter). Ongoing efforts are reclaiming the remnants of the old North Coast logging industry by reconstructing natural dunes and removing non-native plant life. There's also a nice **campground** (800/444-7275).

Fort Bragg

Cruising south along Hwy-1, 40 miles from Leggett and US-101, the first real town you come to is **Fort Bragg** (pop. 6,963), whose burly, blue-collar edge comes as something of a shock on the otherwise undeveloped, touristy Mendocino coast. Formerly home to a large Georgia-Pacific lumber mill (plans to redevelop it are still in the works and may include ecofriendly housing and a shopping and light industrial com-

aerial view of Fort Bragg

plex), and still home to the region's largest commercial fishing fleet, Fort Bragg takes a mostly no-frills approach to the tourist trade, leaving the dainty B&B scene to its upscale neighbor, Mendocino. However, the coastline is lovely, and there are a few down-to-earth places to eat, starting with the very good omelets and other eggy dishes at the appropriately named **Egghead's Restaurant** (326 N. Main St., 707/964-5005). Perhaps the most popular place in town is **North Coast Brewing Co.** (455 N. Main St., 707/964-2739), which serves good food and fine pints of its tasty Red Seal Ale among at least a dozen top-notch brews. As you might expect, Fort Bragg has a number of timeworn bars and taverns, like the **Golden West Saloon** (128 E. Redwood Ave.), two blocks south of the brewery.

Fort Bragg also boasts some unexpected treats: **Cowlick's Ice Cream Café** (250 N. Main St., 707/962-9271) and the best pizza for miles at **D'Aurelios** (438 S. Franklin St., 707/964-4227), a block east of Hwy-1.

Fort Bragg also has at least one exemplar of that rare species, the inexpensive (by Mendocino coast standards, at least) motel: the

Beachcomber Motel (1111 N. Main St., 707/964-2402, $109 and up). Handy for the Ten-Mile Haul Road path, this is pretty much the coast's only beachfront accommodation option (apart from camping).

At the south edge of Fort Bragg, near the Hwy-20 junction and eight miles north of the town of Mendocino, 47 acres of intensely landscaped coastal hillsides tumble down between Hwy-1 and the ocean to form the **Mendocino Coast Botanical Gardens** (707/964-4352, daily, $14 adults), a nonprofit public space showing off the abundance of plant life that thrives in this mild, lush environment. Cultivated varieties like camellias, azaleas, roses, irises, fuchsias, and dahlias share space with native ferns, pines, redwoods, wildflowers, and wetland plants. It's also the only public garden in the continental USA that fronts right onto the ocean, so you can enjoy crashing waves and maybe even watch a gray whale spout offshore.

From Fort Bragg, the **California Western Railroad** (707/964-6371, $54 and up) runs a number of historic steam- and diesel-powered Skunk Trains over the mountains to Willits and back. Half-day and full-day trips run year-round.

Mendocino

Mendocino

One of the prettiest towns on the California coast (as seen in TV shows like *Murder, She Wrote* and numerous movies), **Mendocino** (pop. 894) is an artists' and writers' community par excellence. Now firmly established as an upscale escape for wage-slaving visitors from San Francisco (hence the local nickname, "Spendocino"), the town was originally established as a logging port in the 1850s. In recent years, Mendocino has successfully preserved its rugged sandstone coastline—great for wintertime whale-watching—while converting many of its New England-style clapboard houses into super-quaint B&B inns. The area is ideal for leisurely wandering, following the many paths winding through **Mendocino Headlands State Park**, which wraps around the town and offers uninterrupted views across open fields, heathers, and other coastal flora to the crashing ocean beyond. For field guides, maps, or a look at Mendocino in its lumbering heyday, stop by the visitors center in the historic **Ford House** (735 Main St., 707/937-5397).

Two miles north of town, one of the north coast's most perfect places is protected as **Russian Gulch State Park** (707/937-5804), where a waterfall, a soaring highway bridge, lush inland canyons, a swimming beach, and an impressive blowhole are yours to enjoy along more than a mile of undisturbed coastline. There's camping, too, and sea kayaking, plus a fairly flat, three-mile paved bike trail and miles of hiking.

Along with its many fine art galleries and bookshops, the town of Mendocino also has a delicious collection of bakeries, cafés, and restaurants. If you're not getting a breakfast at a B&B, come to the very friendly **Mendocino Cafe** (10451 Lansing St., 707/937-6141), where locals have been starting their days for more than 20 years. For a total splurge, try one of California's most famous (and expensive!) restaurants, **Cafe Beaujolais** (961 Ukiah St., 707/937-5614, lunch and dinner Wed.-Sun., dinner Mon.-Tues.), two blocks from the waterfront, which serves California cuisine delicacies.

Places to stay in Mendocino are rather expensive but generally delightful. The lovely **MacCallum House Inn** (45020 Albion St., 707/937-0289, $149 and up) includes a beautiful garden, good breakfasts, and a cozy nighttime bar and restaurant. Another place to stay is the circa-1858 **Mendocino Hotel & Garden Suites** (45080 Main St., 707/937-0511, $186 and up), on the downtown waterfront.

Mendocino, as you might expect from a well-heeled artists colony, also has a pretty lively music scene. If you just want to drink and unwind after a long day on the road, head to **Dick's Place** (707/937-6010) at the west end of Main Street.

Van Damme State Park

Three miles south of Mendocino at the mouth of the Little River, **Van Damme State Park** stretches along the coastal bluffs and beaches and includes some 1,800 acres of pine and redwood forest. The park's unique attribute is the oddly contorted **Pygmy Forest,** a natural bonsai-like grove of miniature pines, cypress, and manzanita, with a wheelchair-accessible nature trail explaining the unique ecology. There's also a small, very popular campground, concession-guided ocean kayak tours, and a **visitors center** (707/937-4016) housed in a New Deal-era recreation hall.

The nearby hamlet of **Little River** is home to some rural-feeling, peaceful alternatives to Mendocino's in-town accommodations: the very comfy **Inn at Schoolhouse Creek** (800/731-5525, $179 and up), where quaint cottages sit in nine acres of dog- and child-friendly gardens around a historic, oceanview home; and the luxurious, gourmet food-and-wine indulgence of the **Little River Inn** (707/937-5942, $189 and up during the high season), where five generations of the same family have been welcoming travelers since 1939.

Anderson Valley

From Hwy-1 south of Mendocino, Hwy-128 cuts diagonally across to US-101 through the lovely **Anderson Valley,** home to numerous fine

vineyard in Anderson Valley

wineries (including Husch, Navarro, and Kendall-Jackson) and the *Anderson Valley Advertiser,* one of California's most outspoken local newspapers. Anderson Valley also has its own regional dialect, called "Boontling," combining English, Scots-Irish, Spanish, and Native American words into a lighthearted lingo created, some say, simply to befuddle outsiders—or "shark the bright-lighters," in the local lingo.

To find out more, stop in the valley's tiny main town, **Boonville,** at the All That Good Stuff gift shop and ad hoc information center. Fans of local food and wine will want to cross the highway to the **Boonville Hotel** (14050 Hwy-128, 707/895-2210, $125 and up), which has a wonderful restaurant (dinner only, alas) and wine bar. The historic building has upstairs rooms filled with art and furniture made by local craftspeople. Beer fans can make a pilgrimage east of town (toward Ukiah) to the partially solar-powered home of the **Anderson Valley Brewing Company** (17700 Hwy-253, 707/895-2337), where you can sample some of the world's best beers, including the legendary Boont Amber Ale.

Elk

While the coastal scenery is stupendous all the way along the Mendocino coast, one place worth keeping an eye out for on the drive along Hwy-1 is the tiny roadside community of **Elk** (pop. 250), 15 miles south of Mendocino. Elk is a wonderful little wide-spot-in-the-road, with what must be one of the oldest and most characterful service stations in California (the Elk Garage, in business since 1901) alongside a great little veggie-friendly breakfast-and-lunch road-food stop: **Queenie's Roadhouse Café** (707/877-3285, closed Tues.-Wed.). Elk also boasts a general store, some quirky cliffside cabins, and a steep trail leading down to the Pacific shore at Greenwood Cove. If you have the time and means for a splurge, the peaceful oceanfront **Elk Cove Inn** (707/877-3321, $100 and up) is a delightful small B&B inn.

Point Arena and Gualala

With only a few exceptions, the southernmost 40 miles of Mendocino coastline are almost totally undeveloped and virtually uninhabited, with green forests and coastal coves as far as the eye can see. The westernmost point here, **Point Arena,** is about five miles northwest of Hwy-1 via Lighthouse Road (the namesake lighthouse, built in 1870, stands 115 feet tall). Back on Hwy-1, the small town of Point Arena is worth a wander for nice cafés and bakeries; try the fluffy quiches or buttery croissants at *le très* Francophile **Franny's Cup & Saucer** (213 Main St., 707/882-2500), across the street from the lively Arena Theater, which puts on new-run movies nightly and good live music.

Another 15 miles south, situated at the very southern edge of Mendocino County, the old logging port of **Gualala** (pop. 585) has one truly remarkable feature: the Russian Orthodox domes of **St. Orres** (36601 S. Hwy-1, 707/884-3303), now a B&B inn and $100-a-head gourmet restaurant glowing with polished wood and stained glass, above Hwy-1 on the north side of town.

If you prefer to hang out with locals rather than well-heeled tourists from San Francisco, head instead to local bakeries like **Trinks Café** (707/884-1713) in the Seacliff Center shopping complex, or grab a BBQ brisket sandwich at **Bones Roadhouse** (707/884-1188), just north. Great camping and an incredible coastal panorama can be yours at **Gualala Point Regional Park** (707/785-2377, $7 day entrance, $32 camping), a mile south of town along the Gualala River.

Sea Ranch

Midway between Mendocino and the San Francisco Bay Area, the vacation-home community of **Sea Ranch** was laid out in the mid-1960s by an enthusiastic group of architects and planners, including Lawrence Halprin and the late Charles Moore, who hoped to show that development need not destroy or negatively impact the natural beauty of the California coast. Strict design guidelines, preserving over half the 5,000 acres as open space and requiring the use of muted natural wood cladding and other barn-like features, made it an aesthetic success, which you can appreciate for yourself at the **Sea Ranch Lodge** (707/785-2371, $219 and up), near the south end of the development.

The rest of Sea Ranch, however, is strictly private, which has raised the hackles of area activists, who after years of lawsuits finally forced through a few coastal access trails in the mid-1980s; these, such as **Walk-On Beach** at milepost 56.5, are marked by turnouts along Hwy-1.

Salt Point State Park

The many sheltered rocky coves of **Salt Point State Park** make it ideal for undersea divers, who come to hunt the abundant abalone. Along these six miles of jagged shoreline, pines and redwoods clutch the water's edge, covering some 6,000 acres on both sides of Hwy-1 to make Salt Point a prime place for hiking and camping. For a guide to the 20 miles of trails, or background on the sandstone mortars and other remnants of the Kashaya Pomo tribal village that stood here until the 1850s, contact the **visitors center** (707/847-3221).

One of the few positive effects of cutting down the native redwood forests that once covered the Northern California coast has been the emergence of giant-sized rhododendrons in their place. You'll find the most impressive display at the **Kruse Rhododendron State Natural Preserve,** high above Hwy-1 adjacent to Salt Point State Park, where some 300 acres of rhododendrons, some reaching 14 feet in height, burst forth in late spring, usually peaking around the first week of May.

In between Salt Point and Fort Ross, Beniamino Bufano's 93-foot *Peace* statue looms like a shiny silver missile alongside Hwy-1 above craggy Timber Cove, where there's also a nice **restaurant and inn** (707/847-3231, $171 and up).

Fort Ross State Historic Park

If you're captivated by California's lively history, one of the most evocative spots in the state is **Fort Ross State Historic Park,** the well-restored remains of a Russian fur-trapping outpost built here in 1812. During a 30-year residency, the Russians farmed wheat and potatoes, traded with native tribes, and trapped local seals and

Russian Orthodox chapel at Fort Ross

Bohemian Grove, the world's most exclusive men's club, covers 2,700 acres of redwood forest just south of the Russian River outside the village of Monte Rio.

sea otters for their furs, which commanded huge sums on the European market. By 1840, the near-destruction of the sea otter population caused the company to shut down operations and sell the fort to Sacramento's John Sutter, who financed the purchase on credit.

Later, the abandoned fort was badly damaged by the 1906 San Francisco earthquake and later fires, but the state has completed a high-quality restoration and reconstruction project, using hand-hewn lumber and historically accurate building methods to replicate the original barracks and other buildings, including a luminous redwood chapel.

Fort Ross spreads west from Hwy-1, 20 miles south of Sea Ranch and a dozen miles north of the Russian River. Outside the fort's walls, a modern **visitor center** (707/847-3286, closed Tues.-Wed., $8 per car) traces the site's natural, native, and Russian history, and offers information on the park's many fine hiking trails.

Jenner, Guerneville, and the Russian River

South of Fort Ross, Hwy-1 climbs high above the rugged coastline, offering breathtaking vistas of the Pacific Ocean hundreds of feet below. Twelve miles south of Fort Ross, Hwy-1 reaches the low-key resort community of **Jenner** (pop. 170), which stretches along the broad mouth of the Russian River. Harbor seals and sea lions sun the closing of the Russian River ferry, c. 1931

themselves on the beach at **Goat Rock,** houses climb the steep hillsides, and there's also a gas station, a post office, and the excellent **River's End** (707/865-2484, daily in summer, otherwise closed Wed.), which has a range of great food (everything from burgers to Indonesian-spiced seafood) and oceanview tables (inside and outside, depending on the weather).

From Jenner, Hwy-116 runs east along the river, passing through forests, vineyards, and popular summertime resort towns, the largest of which is **Guerneville,** 13 miles away, with a number of worthwhile cafés and a largely gay and lesbian summer population. A more traditional place, with a broad but gravelly beach, boat rentals, cabins, and riverfront camping, is **Johnson's Beach & Resort** (16241 1st St., 707/869-2022). After 35-odd miles, Hwy-116 eventually links up with the US-101 freeway to and from San Francisco, providing a faster alternative to coastal Hwy-1.

Sonoma Coast State Park

South of Jenner and the Russian River, Hwy-1 hugs the coast along 10 miles of rocky coves and sandy beaches, collectively protected as **Sonoma Coast State Park** (707/875-3483). Starting with Goat Rock at the southern lip of the Russian River mouth, a bluff-top trail leads south past intriguingly named and usually unpopulated pocket strands like Blind Beach, Schoolhouse Beach, Shell Beach, Wright's Beach (site of the park's main beachfront campground), and Salmon Creek Beach.

At the southernmost end, Sonoma Coast State Park broadens to include the wildflower-covered granite promontory of **Bodega Head,** which juts into the Pacific and provides a great vantage point for watching the gray whale migrations in winter.

Bodega Bay

Protected by the massive bulk of Bodega Head, the fishing harbor of **Bodega Bay** has grown into an upscale vacation des-

While hiking along the Sonoma Coast, be careful: Many people have been drowned by "sleeper" waves, which rise unannounced and sweep people off the rocky shore.

tination, with Sea Ranch-style vacation homes lining the fairways of golf resorts and deluxe hotels overlooking the still-busy commercial wharves. On the waterfront, the **Lucas Wharf Restaurant & Bar** (595 S. Hwy-1, 707/875-3522) dishes up fish-and-

Bodega's church, used by Alfred Hitchcock in *The Birds*

chips and clam chowder. Next door, the **Fishetarian Fish Market** (599 S. Hwy-1, 707/875-9092) has fantastic fresh rock cod fish-and-chips, tasty fries, and a large fresh-fish market. If you've had your fill of fish, continue south to the rustic U.S. Post Office and mini-mall west of the highway, where you can enjoy milk shakes and hot dogs at the **Dog House** (707/875-2441).

South of Bodega Bay, Hwy-1 cuts inland around the marshy coastal estuaries, passing by the photogenic small town of **Bodega,** whose Victorian-era hilltop church was used by Alfred Hitchcock for many of the scariest scenes in his 1963 movie, *The Birds.* In 1976, international artists Christo and Jeanne-Claude used Bodega as a key tableau in their installation *Running Fence,* which draped an 18-foot-high, nearly 25-mile-long fabric curtain across the rolling ranchlands of Sonoma County, from the coast to the inland valleys. There's not much sign of Hollywood directors or conceptual art in these parts today, but Bodega is a nice place to wander and explore, and the down-home **Casino Bar** (17000 Bodega Hwy., 707/876-3185) at the center of "town" is more welcoming than it might look, with a well-worn pool table and excellent, locally-sourced food most nights.

Valley Ford

Between Bodega Bay and Point Reyes, Hwy-1 veers inland to avoid the marshy lowlands, and midway between the two bigger destinations the winding two-lane highway brings you to a great road-trip stop. **Valley Ford** is a photogenic community that holds a great, old family-run roadhouse, **Dinucci's** (707/876-3260, dinner only Thurs.-Mon., plus lunch on weekends, $10-20 per person), serving huge portions of unreconstructed Italian food—minestrone, fresh bread, salad, and pasta. More self-consciously stylish, contemporary fare is on the menu next door at quirky **Rocker Oysterfeller's** (707/876-1983, dinner Thurs.-Fri., lunch and dinner Sat., brunch and dinner Sun.), inside the Civil War-era **Valley Ford Hotel,** which has been renovated with luxurious rooms while retaining old-time charm (quilts on the beds, rocking chairs on the porch, the whole nine yards).

Point Reyes

Between Bodega Bay and the Golden Gate Bridge, Hwy-1 slices through one of the country's most scenically and economically wealthy areas, **Marin County.** Though less than an hour from San Francisco, the northwestern reaches of the county are surprisingly rural, consisting of rolling dairylands and a few untouched small towns; Hwy-1 follows a slow and curving route along the usually uncrowded two-lane blacktop.

A sign outside the small white garage on Main Street in Point Reyes Station claims it is the oldest Chevrolet dealer in California.

After looping inland south of Bodega Bay, Hwy-1 reaches the shore again at oyster-rich **Tomales Bay,** around which it winds for a dozen or so miles before reaching the earthy but erudite town of **Point Reyes Station.** Here the excellent **Station House Cafe** (11180 Hwy-1, 415/663-1515, closed Wed.) serves incredibly good breakfasts and delicious lunches that include great-tasting local oysters, on the half-shell or barbecued. The bar is lively and well stocked, and hosts free live music most Sunday afternoons.

Northwest from town along Sir Francis Drake Boulevard, the 70,000-plus-acre **Point Reyes National Seashore** offers an entire guidebook's worth of hiking and cycling trails, broad beaches, dense forests, and more; stop at the **Bear Valley Visitor Center** (415/464-5100, daily, free) for more information. The photogenic lighthouse at the tip of Point Reyes gives great views over the coast, and in winter and spring (Dec.-June) the steep headland makes an ideal spot for watching migrating gray whales.

Eight miles from the visitors center, the **HI-Point Reyes Hostel** (1390 Limantour Spit Rd., 415/663-8811) has dorm beds in an old farmhouse on the road to Drake's Bay.

Dozens of delightful inns and restaurants operate in and around Point Reyes, but because they're a mere 35 miles from San Francisco, they're often booked solid weeks in advance. Everything from treetop rooms to waterfront cabins can be found through the local **chamber of commerce** (415/663-9232, www.pointreyes.org).

Bolinas and Stinson Beach

Sitting at the southern end of the Point Reyes peninsula, **Bolinas** is a small town with a well-earned reputation for discouraging tourists. The signs leading you here from Hwy-1 are regularly torn down by locals bent on keeping the place to themselves. It's blessed with one of the coast's best tide-pool areas in **Duxbury Reef,** which curves around the western edge of Bolinas. The town itself is little more than a general store, a bakery, some cafes, and a bar. The 1850s saloon **Smiley's Schooner** (41 Wharf Rd., 415/868-1311) offers live music and few upstairs rooms.

In contrast, the broad strands of **Stinson Beach,** four miles south of Bolinas along Hwy-1, are the Bay Area's most popular summertime suntanning spots. A grocery store and deli, the **Live Water Surf Shop** (which rents boards and the essential wetsuits), and a couple of outdoor bar-and-grills along Hwy-1 form a short parade at the entrance to the beach. The best place to eat hereabouts is the **Parkside Cafe** (43 Arenal Ave., 415/868-1272). If you want to stay overnight, try the pleasant **Sandpiper Inn** (415/868-1632, $125 and up), just west of Hwy-1.

If you have the chance to plan ahead, try to book a night at the **Steep Ravine Cabins** (800/444-7275, around $100), just over a mile south of Stinson Beach on the ocean side of Hwy-1. Now part of Mt. Tamalpais State Park, these 10 rustic redwood cabins are very basic, roof-over-the-head accommodations (bring sleeping bags and food; water faucets are just outside the door) in an absolutely beautiful coastal chasm. These very popular cabins (originally owned by Bay Area bigwigs like Dorothea Lange) sleep up to five people.

Mt. Tamalpais, Muir Woods, and Muir Beach

From the coast, a pair of roads—Panoramic Highway and the Shoreline Highway (Hwy-1)—twist up and over the slopes of **Mt. Tamalpais** (elev. 2,586), the signature peak of the San Francisco Bay Area. Known usually as "Mt. Tam," the whole mountain has been protected in semi-natural state within a series of state and national parks, and its voluptuous slopes offer incredible views of the urbanized Bay Area and the untouched coastline. Drive to within 100 yards of the top for a 360-degree panorama, or stop at the Pantoll **ranger station** (415/388-2070) for a map of Mt. Tam's hiking routes and fire roads. One of the world's great trails, the Dipsea Trail between Muir Woods and Stinson Beach, hits its highest points and gives its greatest views within a short stroll of the Pantoll parking lot and walk-in campground.

If you plan ahead, you may also be able to spend the night on the mountain, indoors, in the comfort of **The West Point Inn** (415/388-9955, $50 adults), a hiker-centric, walk-in only lodge (two mostly-level miles from Pantoll), that was built back in 1904 as part of a long-vanished scenic railroad, whose right-of-way is now one of Mt. Tam's most popular hiking trails.

A deep, dark valley between the coast and Mt. Tamalpais holds the last surviving stand of Marin County redwoods, preserved for future generations as the **Muir Woods National Monument** (daily 8am-dusk, $7 adults) and named in honor of turn-of-the-20th-century naturalist John Muir. A paved, mile-long trail takes in the biggest trees, but since the park is often crowded with busloads of sightseeing hordes making the tour from San Francisco, you may want to explore the farther-flung areas, climbing up Mt. Tamalpais or following Muir Creek

view from atop Mt. Tamalpais

The all-terrain mountain bike, which now accounts for half of all bikes on (and off) the roads, was invented in the late 1970s by a group of daredevil Marin cyclists intent on cruising down the fire roads of Mt. Tamalpais at the highest possible speed.

two miles downstream to the crescent-shaped cove of **Muir Beach,** along Hwy-1. Besides stunning scenery, Muir Beach is also home to the welcoming **Pelican Inn** (415/383-6000, rooms $225 and up), an "Olde English"-style pub serving food and fine beers; overnight guests get cozy rooms and access to a delightful room called "The Snug," with a fireplace.

Another enjoyably ersatz experience awaits at the junction of Hwy-1 and the US-101 freeway, where a historic roadside restaurant has been resurrected as the **Buckeye Roadhouse** (15 Shoreline Hwy., 415/331-2600), near Mill Valley, where you can feast on fine barbecue, great steaks and burgers, and delicious desserts in a lively, retro-Route 66 atmosphere.

Marin Headlands

If you can avoid the magnetic pull of the Golden Gate Bridge and San Francisco, take the very last turnoff from US-101 (northbound drivers take the second turnoff after crossing the bridge) and head west to the **Marin Headlands,** a former military base that's been turned back into coastal semi-wilderness. A tortuous road twists along the face of 300-foot cliffs, giving incredible views of the bridge and the city behind it. The road continues west and north to the **Visitor Center** (415/331-1540), housed in an old chapel, with a reconstructed Miwok shelter and details on hiking and biking routes. And if you're so inclined, on Wednesday-Friday afternoons and the first Saturday of each month, you can tour the world's only restored Cold War-era **Nike missile silo** (free).

Nearby, the barracks of old Fort Barry have been converted into the very peaceful **HI-Marin Headlands Hostel** (415/331-2777, dorm beds $30 and up), which has dorm beds as well as private rooms.

Across San Francisco

From the north, Hwy-1 enters **San Francisco** across the glorious **Golden Gate Bridge,** where parking areas at both ends let you ditch the car and walk across the elegant 1.7-mile-long span. South from the bridge, Hwy-1 follows 19th Avenue across Golden Gate Park, then runs due south through the outer reaches of San Francisco, finally reaching the coast again at the often-foggy town of Pacifica. The most scenic alternative is the **49-Mile Scenic Drive,** the best part of which heads west from the bridge through the **Presidio,** along Lincoln Boulevard and Camino del Mar, following the rugged coastline to **Lands End,** where you can hike around and explore the remains of Sutro Baths, eat a burger or grilled cheese at **Louis'** (415/387-6330), a historic diner with amazing views, or dine at the wonderful (and not all-that-expensive) **Cliff House** (415/386-3330).

Every June since 1905, one of the country's wildest foot races, the **Dipsea** (415/331-3550), has followed a rugged 7.4-mile route from the town of Mill Valley to Stinson Beach.

From Lands End, this scenic route runs south along the ocean-front Great Highway, which eventually links back up with Hwy-1 near the small but enjoyable **San Francisco Zoo** (415/753-7080, daily, $18 adults).

Since driving and parking in San Francisco can be frustrating and expensive (Steve McQueen could never make *Bullitt* in today's traffic!), consider parking out here in the 'burbs and taking public transportation into the center of town. The N Judah Muni trolley line runs between downtown and the coast just south of Golden Gate Park, via the Sunset District neighborhood, where parking is comparatively plentiful.

Montara and Princeton

From the San Francisco city limits, Hwy-1 runs along the Pacific Ocean through the rural and almost totally undeveloped coastline of San Mateo County. The first eight miles or so are high-speed freeway, but after passing through the suburban communities of **Daly City** and **Pacifica,** the pace abruptly slows to a scenic cruise. Pacifica, which has a long pier, a popular surfing beach, a bowling alley, an oceanview Taco Bell, and a handy Holiday Inn Express motel, makes a good edge-of-town base for seeing the San Francisco area. South of Pacifica, two-lane Hwy-1 hugs the decomposing cliff tops of **Devil's Slide,** where the terrifying old highway is being converted into a cycling and hiking path following completion of a long-delayed new tunnel (decades in the making).

The first real place south of Pacifica is the ramshackle beach town of **Montara,** where the old but still functioning lighthouse

San Francisco

San Francisco is easily the most enjoyable city in the United States. Its undulating topography turns every other corner into a scenic vista, while its many distinctive neighborhoods are perfect for aimless wandering. Museums document everything from Gold Rush history to cutting-edge modern art, while stellar restaurants offer the chance to sample gourmet food from around the world—all in an easily manageable, densely compact small city.

view from inside Fort Point, with the Golden Gate Bridge overhead

If there's one place in the city you should stop to get your bearings, it's **Fort Point,** a massive, photogenic Civil War fort standing along the bay, directly beneath the Golden Gate Bridge. You can wander at will through the honeycomb of corridors, staircases, and gun ports, watch the fearless surfers and windsurfers offshore, and take in a panoramic view of the City by the Bay. From here you can walk up to and across the **Golden Gate Bridge,** or head west to **Land's End** or back into town via a popular bayfront walking and cycling trail. Another great place to get a feel for San Francisco is **Golden Gate Park,** which stretches inland from the western edge of the city, including more than 1,000 acres of gardens, a boating lake, and two landmark museums, featuring the copper-clad art of the **de Young Museum,** and the natural history, aquarium, and planetarium of the grass-roofed **California Academy of Sciences.**

If there's one other place that ought to be on your S.F. itinerary, it's **Alcatraz.** Aptly known as The Rock, this was America's most notorious

the Conservatory of Flowers in Golden Gate Park

prison from 1934 until 1963. Now preserved as a historical park, the island is worth a visit as much for the views of San Francisco as for its grim past. To reach Alcatraz, take one of the ferries that leave throughout the day from Pier 41 at the east end of Fisherman's Wharf.

The **San Francisco Giants** (877/4SF-4849, tickets around $25 and up) play at retro-modern AT&T Park, along the bay in downtown's South of Market district.

PRACTICALITIES

San Francisco is one of the few cities on the West Coast where you really don't need a car, since distances are short and public transportation is quite extensive; the grid street plan makes it easy to find your way around. San Francisco's **Municipal Railway** ("Muni"; 415/673-6864) network of public transit buses, trams, and cable cars will take you all over the city.

The only problem for visitors in San Francisco is deciding where to eat–there are so many great places that choosing among them can be a painful process. For breakfast, **Sears Fine Foods** (439 Powell St., 415/986-0700) on Union Square is a local institution, as is the upscale **Fog City** (1300 Battery St., 415/982-2000), which serves gourmet comfort food (and the world's best French toast on weekends). Two more S.F. culinary landmarks are the **Swan Oyster Depot** (1517 Polk St., 415/673-1101 or 415/673-2757, Mon.-Sat. till 5:30pm only), a half block north of the California Street cable car, a simple oyster bar serving the city's freshest shellfish and coldest Anchor Steam beer; and **Sam's Grill** (374 Bush St., 415/421-0594), downtown, with incredible grilled meat and fish dishes, melt-in-your-mouth shoestring fries, and ancient-looking 1930s wooden booths that seem like set pieces from a Sam Spade mystery.

Given San Francisco's worldwide popularity, it's no surprise that room rates run pretty high–expect to pay $250 a night or more (plus parking and taxes). If you're here for a honeymoon or other romantic reason, the nicest place in town is the swanky **Mandarin Oriental** (222 Sansome St., 415/276-9888, $450 and up), which fills the top floors of a Financial District skyscraper and has 270-degree bay views (even from the bathtubs!). The best budget options are three **HI hostels,** one on the bay at Fort Mason (415/771-7277), another downtown (312 Mason St., 415/788-5604), and a third near Civic Center (685 Ellis St., 415/474-5721). Each one costs about $30 a night, $90 for a private room. In between there are some nice motels on the outskirts of downtown, like the nouveau retro **Hotel del Sol** (3100 Webster St., 415/921-5520, $149 and up), in the Marina District.

The **San Francisco Visitor Information Center** (415/391-2000) publishes a good free street map and offers extensive listings of attractions, accommodations, and restaurants.

has been partly converted into the **HI-Point Montara Lighthouse Hostel** (650/728-7177).

South of Montara, Hwy-1 bends inland around the rugged shores of the **Fitzgerald Marine Reserve** (650/728-3584), a wonderful (but very frag-

the opening of the Golden Gate Bridge, 1937

ile) tide pool area filled with anemones and other delicate sea creatures. The tide pools are visible at low tide only; look, but don't touch! Hwy-1 continues south past the Pillar Point Harbor at **Princeton-by-the-Sea,** where you can enjoy a different sort of seal-ife appreciation: the fresh fish-and-chips (plus nice wines and cold beers) at **Barbara's Fishtrap** (650/728-7049, cash only).

Half Moon Bay

The first sizable coastal town south of San Francisco, **Half Moon Bay** (pop. 11,324) is 25 miles from the city but seems much more distant. A quiet farming community that's slowly but surely changing into a Silicon Valley exurb, Half Moon Bay still has an all-American Main Street lined by hardware stores, cafés, bakeries, and the inevitable art galleries and B&Bs. The main event hereabouts is the annual **Art & Pumpkin Festival,** held mid-October, which celebrates the coming of Halloween with a competition to determine the world's largest pumpkin—winning gourds weigh more than 1,500 pounds!

Until the construction of the $500-a-night beachfront Ritz-Carlton golf resort, the coastline of Half Moon Bay was almost completely undeveloped, but it's still pretty nice and accessible, with a four-mile-long string of state park beaches at the foot of bluff-top vegetable farms and horse ranches. The town also retains its rural feel. But thanks to the presence of so many Silicon Valley billionaires just over the hills, it has significantly better restaurants. The best fish tacos (and great fish-and-chips) can be had at the **Flying Fish Bar & Grill** (650/712-1125), off Hwy-92 at the north end of Main Street. Excellent and not outrageously expensive Italian specialties are on the menu at **Pasta Moon** (315 Main St., 650/726-5125).

Pescadero and Pigeon Point Lighthouse

The 50 miles of coastline between Half Moon Bay and Santa Cruz are one of the great surprises of the California coast: The virtually unspoiled miles offer rocky tide pools and driftwood-strewn beaches beneath sculpted bluffs topped by rolling green fields of brussels sprout, artichokes, and U-pick berry patches. Access to the water is not always very easy, and while surfers seem to park along Hwy-1 and walk across the fields to wherever the waves are breaking, for visitors it's best to aim for one of the half dozen state parks, like San Gregorio, Pomponio, Bean Hollow, or Año Nuevo.

The biggest town hereabouts, **Pescadero** (pop. 643) is a mile or so inland from Hwy-1 and well worth the short detour for a chance to sample the fresh fish, great pies, and other home-cooked treats at **Duarte's Tavern** (202 Stage Rd., 650/879-0464, daily breakfast, lunch, and dinner), at the south end of the block-long downtown.

Looking for the world's biggest waves? Head down to **Mavericks,** an offshore reef area off Pillar Point, three miles north of Half Moon Bay. In winter, when conditions are right, mega-waves as high as 80 feet draw expert surfers from all over the world. For a report, and a safety advisory to warn off any wannabes, call **Mavericks Surf Shop** (650/560-8088); it's located at Pillar Point Harbor, as near as you can get to the offshore breaks.

Less than 10 miles south of Pescadero, the photogenic beacon of **Pigeon Point Lighthouse** has appeared in innumerable TV and print commercials. The graceful, 115-foot-tall brick tower is closed, but the grounds are open for **tours** (Fri.-Mon. 10am-4pm, donation), and the adjacent lighthouse quarters function as the

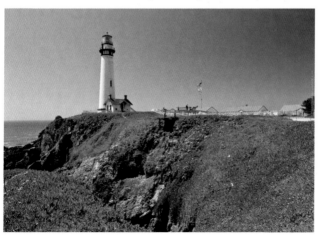

Pigeon Point Lighthouse

very popular **HI-Pigeon Point Lighthouse Hostel** (650/879-0633), which has dorms beds, family-friendly private rooms, and a hot tub perched above the crashing surf.

Año Nuevo State Reserve

West of Hwy-1, one of nature's more bizarre spectacles takes place annually at **Año Nuevo State Park** (650/879-0227, daily 8am-dusk), where each winter hundreds of humongous northern elephant seals come ashore to give birth and mate. The males reach up to 13 feet head-to-tail, weigh as much as 4,500 pounds, and have dangling proboscises that inspired their name. These blubbery creatures were hunted almost to extinction for their oil-rich flesh. In 1910, fewer than 100 were left in the world; their resurgence to a current population of more than 100,000 has proved that protection does work.

Every December, after spending the summer at sea, hordes of male elephant seals arrive here at Año Nuevo, the seals' primary onshore rookery, ready to do battle with each other for the right to procreate. It's an incredible show, with the bulls bellowing, barking, and biting at each other to establish dominance; the "alpha male" mates with most of the females, and the rest must wait till next year. Pups conceived the previous year are born in January, and mating goes on through March. During the mating season, ranger-led **tours** (800/444-4445, $7) are the only way to see the seals; these tours are very popular, so plan ahead and try to come midweek. The three-mile walk from the parking area to the shore is worth doing at any time of year, since it's a very pretty scene and some of the seals are residents year-round.

The only accommodation option along this stretch of coast is three miles south of the lighthouse, or two miles north of the entrance to Año Nuevo, at **Costanoa** (650/879-1100, $80 and up). A stylish retro-modern eco-minded resort, open since 1999 on the inland side of Hwy-1, Costanoa has everything from a luxurious lodge to tent cabins (complete with saunas!). There's also a bar and grill and an adjacent **KOA campground** (650/879-7302).

South of Ano Nuevo State Park, you'll see signs tempting you to stop at **Pie Ranch** (650/879-0995), a rustic roadside attraction selling, you guessed it, fresh pies. They also serve as an ad-hoc education center, hosting weekend potluck dinners and barn dances to spread the word to Silicon Valley denizens about good food and old-fashioned ways of life. As their T-shirts say, "Eat Pie. Teach Pie. Share the Pie." Repeat.

Davenport

Midway between Año Nuevo State Reserve and Santa Cruz, the tiny roadside hamlet of **Davenport** was the birthplace of Odwalla, the fresh-fruit-juice company, beloved of Apple Computer founder Steve Jobs and now owned and run by beverage giant Coca-Cola. The town is a popular stop for cyclists, motorcyclists, and road-tripping Sunday drivers from all over the Bay Area. They come for the strong coffee, diner-style breakfasts, and excellent pastries at the friendly **Whale City Bakery** (490 Coast Rd., 831/423-9009) and the more refined meals and bed-and-breakfast rooms at the neighboring **Davenport Roadhouse at the Cash Store** (831/426-8801).

Two miles north of Davenport, **Swanton Berry Farm** (831/469-8804) is one of the last pick-your-own farms on the California coast. Swanton is also a world leader in truly sustainable agriculture, using biodynamic farming practices and paying the workers union wages while partnering with local markets (and the national chain Whole Foods) to provide the freshest, healthiest produce. And if you don't have the time or inclination to get out in the fields, Swanton's has a farm stand where they sell their delicious fresh berries (and kiwis and brussels sprout, depending upon the season). The famous fruit pies are available year-round.

Big Basin Redwoods State Park

The oldest of California's state parks, **Big Basin Redwoods State Park** (831/338-8860) protects some 18,000 acres of giant coastal redwoods. Established in 1902, the park has many miles of hiking

and cycling trails high up in the mountains. The heart of the park is most easily accessible from Santa Cruz via Hwy-236, but a popular trail winds up from the coast to the crest, starting from Hwy-1 at **Waddell Beach,** a popular haunt for kite-surfers and sailboarders, who sometimes do flips and loops in the wind-whipped waves.

Santa Cruz

The popular beach resort and college town of **Santa Cruz** (pop. 55,600) sits at the north end of Monterey Bay, a 90-minute drive from San Francisco, at the foot of a 3,000-foot-high ridge of mountains. It's best known for its Boardwalk amusement park, which holds the oldest surviving wooden roller coaster on the West Coast, and for the large University of California campus in the redwoods above. The city was named by Spanish explorer Gaspar de Portolá and shares the name Santa Cruz ("holy cross" in Spanish) with the ill-fated mission settlement begun here in 1777. Modern Santa Cruz was all but leveled by an earthquake in 1989 but has since recovered its stature as one of the more diverting stops on the California coast.

Natural Bridges State Beach, four miles south of Santa Cruz via West Cliff Drive, has a natural wave-carved archway and, in winter, swarms of monarch butterflies.

The downtown area lies a mile inland, so from Hwy-1 follow the many signs pointing visitors toward the wharf and the beach, where plentiful parking is available. Walk, rent a bike, or drive along the coastal Cliff Drive to the world's first **Surfing Museum** (in summer Wed.-Mon. 10am-5pm, the rest of the year Thurs.-Mon. noon-4pm, donations), which is packed with giant old redwood boards and newer high-tech cutters, as well as odds and ends tracing the development of West Coast surfing. Housed in an old lighthouse, it overlooks one of the state's prime surfing spots, Steamer Lane, named for the steamships that once brought day-tripping San Franciscans to the wharf.

A large part of the Santa Cruz economy still depends upon visitors, and there are plenty of cafés, restaurants, and accommodation options to choose from. Eating and drinking places congregate east of Hwy-1 along Front Street and Pacific Avenue in downtown Santa Cruz, which has a number of engaging, somewhat countercultural book and record shops along with cafés like **Zoccoli's** (1534 Pacific Ave., 831/423-1711), which has great soups and sandwiches. The best

Surfboard designs have come a long way.

burgers, veggie burgers, and fries are a block west of Pacific at **Jack's Hamburgers** (202 Lincoln St., 831/423-4421). More good veggie food can be had at the **Saturn Café** (145 Laurel St., 831/429-8505), while the stylish **Soif** (105 Walnut Ave., 831/423-2020) has fine wines and tasty tapas-like treats.

Motels line Hwy-1, and some nice-looking Victorian-era B&Bs stand atop Beach Hill, between the Boardwalk and downtown, where the **Seaway Inn** (176 W. Cliff Dr., 831/471-9004, $90 and up) is nice, clean, and reasonably priced. You can also avail yourself of the **HI-Santa Cruz Hostel** (321 Main St., 831/423-8304, dorm beds less than $30) in an immaculate 1870s cottage. Among the many nice B&Bs is the rustic **The Babbling Brook Inn** (1025 Laurel St., 831/427-2437 or 800/866-1131, $190 and up).

Santa Cruz Beach Boardwalk

The bayfront **Santa Cruz Beach Boardwalk** (831/423-5590, daily in summer, weekends the rest of the year, free, rides vary in cost, all-day ride pass around $30) should really be your main stop. Besides the dozens of thrill rides and midway games, it boasts the art deco Cocoanut Grove ballroom and two rides that are such classics of the genre they've been listed as a National Historic Landmark. The biggest thrill is the **Giant Dipper** roller coaster ($6), open since 1924, a senior citizen compared to modern rides but still one of the top coasters in the country—the clattering, half-mile-long tracks make it seem far faster than the 55 mph maximum it reaches. Near the roller coaster is the beautiful Charles

Santa Cruz Beach Boardwalk

Looff **carousel,** one of only six left in the country, with 73 hand-carved wooden horses doing the same circuit they've followed since 1911; grab for the brass rings while listening to music pumped out by the 342-pipe organ, imported from Germany and over 100 years old.

Along with these and many other vintage arcade attractions, the amusement park also features a log flume ride, a sky ride, a two-story miniature-golf course installed inside the old bathhouse, plus a bowling alley and all the shooting galleries, laser tag, and virtual reality machines you could want. The Boardwalk has a concrete concourse but retains a great deal of charm and character.

Mystery Spot

In the hills above Santa Cruz, two miles north of Hwy-1, the **Mystery Spot** (465 Mystery Spot Rd., 831/423-8897, daily, $6 per person and $5 per car) is one of those fortunate few tourist traps that actually get people to come back again. Like similar places along the Pacific Coast, the Mystery Spot is a section of redwood forest where the usual laws of physics seem not to apply (trees grow in oddly contorted corkscrew shapes, and balls roll uphill). Among those who study vortexes and other odd geomantic places, the Mystery Spot is considered to be the real thing, but you don't have to take it seriously to enjoy yourself.

Watsonville, Castroville, and Moss Landing

Between Santa Cruz and Monterey, Hwy-1 loops inland through the farmlands fronting Monterey Bay. Part freeway, part winding two-lane road, Hwy-1 races through, and to be honest there's not a lot worth stopping for: The beaches can be dreary, and the two main towns, **Watsonville** and **Castroville,** are little more than service centers for the local fruit and vegetable packers, though Castroville does have one odd sight: the "World's Largest Artichoke," a concrete statue outside a very large fruit stand at the center of town.

Back on the coast, midway along Monterey Bay, the port community of **Moss Landing** is a busy commercial fishery, with lots of trawlers and packing plants—not to mention pelicans aplenty. Moss Landing sits alongside **Elkhorn Slough,** the largest and most wildlife-rich wetlands area in Monterey Bay (a busy nursery for baby seals, baby otters, and baby leopard

Coastal farms along Monterey Bay grow about 75 percent of the nation's artichokes, which you can sample along with other produce at stands along Hwy-1.

© AVALON TRAVEL

In 1947, then-unknown Marilyn Monroe reigned as Miss Artichoke during Castroville's Artichoke Festival, still celebrated each May.

sharks), which you can see in greatest comfort via **pontoon boat tour** (831/633-5555). Moss Landing is also home to the research arm of the Monterey Bay Aquarium, a nice KOA campground, an obtrusively huge electricity generating plant, and **The Whole Enchilada** (831/633-3038), which has spicy seafood right on Hwy-1, near the power plant. Alternatively, try the sustainable and organic **Haute Enchilada** (7902 Moss Landing Rd., 831/633-5843), west of the highway.

Much of the bayfront north of Monterey formerly belonged to the U.S. Marine Corps base at Fort Ord. Almost the entire parcel was turned over to the State of California to house the **California State University at Monterey Bay,** which opened its doors in 1994.

San Juan Bautista

Away from the coast, 15 miles inland from Monterey Bay via Hwy-129 or Hwy-156, stands one of California's most idyllic small towns, **San Juan Bautista** (pop. 1,862). It centers upon a grassy town square bordered by a well-preserved mission complex, complete with a large church and monastery, standing since 1812. Two other sides of the square are lined by hotels, stables, and houses dating from the 1840s through 1860s, preserved in their entirety within a **state historic park** (831/623-4881, daily).

) Completing the living history lesson, the east edge of the square is formed by one of the state's few preserved stretches of El Camino Real, the 200-year-old Spanish colonial trail that linked all the California missions with Mexico. Adding to the interest, the trail runs right along the rift zone of the San Andreas Fault, and a small seismograph registers tectonic activity. (Incidentally, San Juan Bautista was where the climactic final scenes of Hitchcock's *Vertigo* were filmed—though in the movie, they added a much more prominent bell tower with a seemingly endless staircase.)

The town's main street is a block from the mission and is lined by a handful of antiques shops, Mexican restaurants, and cafés like the **Mission Cafe** (300 3rd St., 831/623-2220).

Monterey

The historic capital of California under the Spanish and Mexican regimes, **Monterey** (pop. 27,810), along with its peninsular neighbors Carmel and Pacific Grove, is one of the most satisfying stops in California. Dozens of significant historical sites have been well preserved, most of them concentrated within a two-mile-long walk called the Path of History that loops through the compact downtown area. Park in the lots at the foot of Alvarado Street, Monterey's main drag, and start your tour at **Fisherman's Wharf,** where bellowing sea lions wallow in the water, begging for popcorn from tourists. Next stop should be the adjacent **Custom House,** the oldest governmental building in the state.

From the Custom House, which is now surrounded by the Portola Hotel & Spa, you can follow the old railroad right-of-way west along the water to **Cannery Row,** where abandoned fish canneries have been gussied up into upscale bars and restaurants—most of them capitalizing on ersatz Steinbeckian themes. The one real attraction here is the excellent **Monterey Bay Aquarium** (886 Cannery Row, 831/648-4800, daily, $40 adults), housed in a spacious modern building and loaded with state-of-the-art tanks filled with over 500 species of local sealife. The aquarium is rated by many as the best in the world: Displays let visitors touch tide-pool denizens, watch playful sea otters, gaze into the gently swaying stalks of a three-story-tall kelp forest, be hypnotized by brilliantly colored jellyfish, or face truly weird creatures that usually live thousands of feet below the surface of the bay.

The internationally-famous **Monterey Jazz Festival** (831/373-3366) is held every September.

jellyfish at the Monterey Bay Aquarium

Map labels:

Point Pinos
Monterey
Monterey Bay
PACIFIC OCEAN
POINT PINOS LIGHTHOUSE
ASILOMAR
PACIFIC GROVE
MONTEREY BAY AQUARIUM
CANNERY ROW
PACIFIC GROVE GATE
68
COUNTRY CLUB GATE
Point Joe
Presidio of Monterey
FISHERMAN'S WHARF
CUSTOM HOUSE
S.F.B. MORSE GATE
MONTEREY
El Estero
17 MILE DRIVE
Forest Lake
Bird Rock
Seal Rock
1
Cypress Point
CYPRESS POINT CLUB
PEBBLE BEACH
68
HWY. 1 GATE
PEBBLE BEACH LINKS
LONE CYPRESS
Stillwater Cove
Pescadero Point
CARMEL GATE
CARMEL
1
Carmel Bay
City Beach
MISSION SAN CARLOS BORROMEO DEL RIO CARMELO
ROBINSON JEFFERS TOR HOUSE
Carmel River
0   1 mile
0   1 kilometer
© AVALON TRAVEL
N

Monterey Practicalities

Because Monterey gets such a considerable tourist trade, there's no shortage of restaurants, though good food at reasonable prices can be hard to find. In the historic center of town, one good bet is the **Old Monterey Café** (489 Alvarado St., 831/646-1021), serving large portions at breakfast and lunch. For breakfast near the aquarium, try **First Awakenings** (125 Oceanview Blvd., 831/372-1125). For seafood, catch an early-bird special (before 6pm) at one of the dozen restaurants on the wharf, or head a mile west along the

Hotel Del Monte, California, on Road of a Thousand Wonders

Along Hwy-1 on the northwest edge of Monterey, the elegant **Club Del Monte,** a grand resort that attracted the first wealthy tourists in the 1880s when it was called Hotel Del Monte, is now part of the large U.S. Naval Postgraduate School.

frontage road to the very popular **Monterey's Fish House** (2114 Del Monte Ave., 831/373-4647).

Places to stay vary widely, starting with the **HI-Monterey Hostel** (778 Hawthorne St., 831/649-0375, $30 and up per person), in historic Carpenters Union Hall off Cannery Row, five blocks from the aquarium. Moderate motels line Munras Street along the old US-101 highway frontage south toward Carmel, while prices in downtown Monterey hover in the $200 range. One exception to the generally high prices is the refurbished and centrally located **Monterey Hotel** (406 Alvarado St., 831/375-3184 or 800/966-6490, $159 and up).

Many other nice places to stay and eat can be found in neighboring Pacific Grove or Carmel. For additional information on destinations from Monterey south to Big Sur, contact the Monterey County **visitors bureau** (831/649-6400 or 1-877-MONTEREY).

Pacific Grove

Perched at the tip of the Monterey Peninsula, **Pacific Grove** (pop. 15,041) is a quiet throwback to old-time tourism, dating from the 1870s when the area was used for summertime Methodist revival meetings. The revivalists' tents and camps later grew into the West Coast headquarters of the populist Chautauqua educational movement, based in upstate New York. The town still has a curiously Midwestern feel, from its many small churches to the rows of well-maintained Victorian cottages lining its quiet streets. Besides the many fine old buildings, the best reason to come here is the beautiful, fully accessible shoreline, which boasts some of the coast's best tide pools, sunset views, and endless opportunities for winter whale-watching.

Pacific Grove's main street, Lighthouse Avenue, runs through the 15-mph commercial district of cafés, galleries, movie theaters, and a small but excellent **Pacific Grove Museum of Natural History** (closed Mon., $8.95 adults), which is a great option for kids or when the weather turns bad. Nearby **Peppers Mexicali Cafe** (170

Forest Ave., 831/373-6892) serves very good, fresh Mexican food, while a range of fairly priced fish dishes are on the menu at **Fishwife** (1996 Sunset Dr., 831/375-7107), near Asilomar, overlooking the wetsuited surfers riding the waves at **Asilomar State Beach.**

Places to stay in Pacific Grove are more reasonably priced than in Monterey or Carmel. **Andril Fireplace Cottages** (569 Asilomar Ave., 831/375-0994, $85 and up) is a lovingly maintained set of old-fashioned motor-court cabins, all with fireplaces and just two blocks from the ocean. The real landmark place to stay is the rustic **Asilomar Conference Grounds** (800 Asilomar Ave., 831/372-8016, $109 and up), on the coast, which has a lovely main lobby (with roaring stone fireplace and heirloom pool tables) and some lovely, woodsy, Julia Morgan-designed cabins and lodge rooms; it is often filled with church groups or convention-goers. For a romantic getaway, it's hard to beat a Victorian-era B&B overlooking the Pacific from Lover's Point: **Seven Gables Inn** (555 Ocean View Blvd., 831/372-4341, $219 and up).

The 17-Mile Drive and Pebble Beach

Spanning the coast between Pacific Grove and Carmel, the **17-Mile Drive** is one of the most famous toll roads in the nation. Opened in the 1880s, the route initially took guests of Monterey's posh Hotel Del Monte on a scenic carriage ride along the coast through the newly planted Del Monte Forest between Carmel and Pacific Grove. Guided by Samuel F. B. Morse, son of the inventor, the formerly wild area underwent devel-

NATIONAL STEINBECK CENTER

The writer John Steinbeck lived in and around the Monterey Peninsula for many years and set many of his stories here, though things have changed so much in recent years that his beloved **Cannery Row** is hard to recognize. Steinbeck was born and is interred in **Salinas,** east of Monterey on US-101; after spurning him for most of his lifetime, the town in 1998 opened the **National Steinbeck Center** (1 S. Main St.) as a memorial to its literary son.

Pacific Grove is the best known of about 20 places in California where millions of migratory monarch butterflies spend the winter months. From October until March, the butterflies congregate on the Butterfly Trees, a grove of pines on Ridge Road off Lighthouse Avenue, well signed from downtown.

opment beginning in the 1920s, first with golf courses like Pebble Beach and Cypress Point, and since then with resort hotels and posh homes.

Enter the drive at any of the gates, where you'll pay the toll (about $10; bicyclists are free, and motorcyclists are banned) and be given a map and guide to the route, pointing out all the scenic highlights, especially the trussed-up old **Lone Cypress,** legally trademarked subject of so many Carmel postcards. It's definitely worth doing the drive, if only to say you have, but to be honest, the views from the drive are no more or less splendid than they are from the toll-free drives, like Ocean View Boulevard in Pacific Grove, Scenic Road in Carmel, or Hwy-1 through Big Sur.

The annual golf tournament hosted by Bing Crosby brought Pebble Beach to national attention. Originally an informal get-together, it grew into one of the main events of the professional circuit and is now the **AT&T Pebble Beach National Pro-Am,** held each winter.

You do, however, get to stop at the Lodge, where your toll will be deducted from the price of lunch or dinner. If you're in the mood to splurge on wanton luxury, you can also stay overnight at either of two extremely plush golf and tennis resorts: the modern, suburban-style country club of **The Inn at Spanish Bay** (1700 17-Mile Dr., 831/647-7500 or 800/654-9300), which is also home to an Ansel Adams photography gallery, or the stately, old-money **Lodge at Pebble Beach** (1700 17-Mile Dr., 831/647-7500 or 800/654-9300). Both resorts charge upwards of $600 a night; for details on accommodations (or Pebble Beach golf fees and tee times), call 800/654-9300.

Carmel

The exclusive enclave of **Carmel-by-the-Sea** (to give its complete name) began life in the early years of the 20th century as a small but lively bohemian colony inhabited by the literary likes of Sinclair Lewis, Mary Austin, and Upton Sinclair. However, with a few arts-and-craftsy exceptions, by the 1950s Carmel had turned into the archly conservative and contrivedly quaint community it is today—a place where Marie Antoinette would no doubt feel at home, dressing down as a peasant, albeit in Chaps by Ralph Lauren. Preserving its rural feel by banning street addresses (and home mail delivery), Carmel simultaneously loves and abhors the many thousands of tourists who descend on it every weekend to window-shop its many designer boutiques and galleries, which fill the few blocks off Ocean Avenue, the main drag through town. Though most of Carmel's many art galleries seem directed at interior decorators, a few are worth searching out, including the **Photography West Gallery** on the southeast corner of Dolores and Ocean, and the **Weston Gallery** on Sixth Avenue near Dolores Street, featuring the works of Edward Weston, Ansel Adams, and other Carmel-based photographers.

Every August for more than 60 years, Pebble Beach has drawn classic car collectors from around the world to show off their immaculately restored automobiles at the annual **Pebble Beach Concours d'Elegance.**

Carmel's leading light, Clint Eastwood, seems ever-present: Besides once serving as mayor, he owns the Mission Ranch resort. As a filmmaker, he used Carmel as the location for one of his most disturbing movies, the psychopathic 1970s *Play Misty for Me.*

Though it's easy to be put off by the surface glitz, Carmel does have a lot going for it. The water is too cold and treacherous for swimming, but broad **Carmel Beach City Park** at the foot of Ocean Avenue gleams white against a truly azure cove. To the south, aptly named **Scenic Road** winds along the rocky coast, past poet Robinson Jeffers's dra-

matic **Tor House** (831/624-1813, tours Fri.-Sat. 10am-3pm, $10). Jeffers, who lived at the house between 1919 and 1962, built much of what you see here out of boulders he hauled up by hand from the beach.

At the south end of the Carmel peninsula, another broad beach, **Carmel River State Beach,** spreads at the mouth of the Carmel River; this usually unpopulated spot is also a favorite spot for scuba divers exploring the deep undersea canyon.

Above the beach, just west of Hwy-1 a mile south of central Carmel, Carmel Mission (daily, $6.50 donation), also known as San Carlos Borroméo de Carmelo, was the most important of all

DRIVING BIG SUR

Stretching 90 miles south of Carmel from Point Lobos all the way to Hearst Castle, Big Sur is one of the most memorable sections of coastline on the planet, with 5,000-foot-tall mountains rising up from the Pacific Ocean. Early Spanish missionaries dubbed it El País Grande del Sur (the Big Country of the South), and the rugged land has resisted development or even much of a population—the current total of around 1,000 is roughly the same as it was in 1900, and for the 3,000 years before that.

Hwy-1, the breathtaking drive through Big Sur, was finally cut across the very steep cliffs in 1937 after 20 years of labor and several fatalities. California's longest and most popular scenic route, it's an incredible trip. Like the Grand Canyon and other larger-than-life natural wonders, Big Sur boggles the mind and, in an odd way, can be hard to handle; you have to content yourself with staring in awestruck appreciation, taking pictures, or maybe toasting the natural handiwork with a cold beer or glass of wine at one of the few but unforgettable cafés and restaurants along the way.

However beautiful the drive along Hwy-1, it's also narrow, twisting, packed with sluggish RVers on holiday weekends, and every few years is closed by mud slides and washouts after torrential winter storms and the even more destructive wildfires that have plagued the coast in recent summers.

Big Sur is still a very wild place (with little or no cell phone reception), and there are very few services, with most of the overnight accommodations booked up solidly during the peak summer season. Spring brings wildflowers, while fall gets the most reliably good weather. No matter when you come, even if you just drive through in an afternoon, be sure to stop whenever possible and get out of the car; scenic viewpoints line the roadside, and dozens of trails lead off into the wilds.

the California missions, serving as home, headquarters, and final resting place of Father Junípero Serra, the Franciscan priest who established Carmel and many of the 20 other California missions, and who is entombed under the chapel floor. The gardens—where on weekends wedding parties alight from limos to take family photos—are beautiful, as is the facade with its photogenic bell tower. This is the mission to visit if you visit only one.

Carmel Practicalities

Dozens of good and usually expensive restaurants thrive in Carmel. One place to see, even if you don't eat there, is the tiny, mock-Tudor **The Tuck Box** (831/624-6365, daily), on Dolores Street near 7th Avenue. Dollhouse-cute, it serves up bacon-and-eggs breakfasts and dainty plates of shepherd's pie and meatloaf for lunch. If you'd rather join locals than mingle with your fellow tourists, head to **Katy's Place** (831/624-0199, daily 7am-2pm) on Mission Street between 5th and 6th, serving delicious waffles and some of the world's best eggs Benedict.

Carmel hotel rates average well over $250 a night, and there isn't any real budget option (apart from nearby Monterey). However, if you want to splurge on a bit of luxury, Carmel is a good place to do it. Besides the golf course resorts of nearby Pebble Beach, Carmel also has the commodious, 1920s-era, mission-style **Cypress Inn** (831/624-3871, $245 and up) at Lincoln and 7th, partly owned by dog-loving Doris Day (and featuring posters of her movies in the small bar off the lobby). A relaxing spot away from downtown is the historic, Clint Eastwood-owned **Mission Ranch** (26270 Dolores St., 831/624-6436 or 800/538-8221, $125 and up), within walking distance of the beach and mission and offering full resort facilities and a very good restaurant.

Point Lobos State Natural Reserve

The sculpted headland south of Carmel Bay, now protected as **Point Lobos State Natural Reserve** (831/624-4909, daily, $10 per car), holds one of the few remaining groves of native Monterey cypress, gnarled and bent by the often stormy coastal weather. The name comes from the barking sea lions (*lobos del mar*) found here by early Spanish explorers; hundreds of seabirds, sea lions, sea otters, and—in winter—gray whales are seen offshore or in the many picturesque, sea-carved coves.

The entrance to the reserve is along Hwy-1, three miles south of Carmel Mission. In summer the park is so popular that visitors

sometimes have to wait in line outside the gates. If possible, plan to come early or during the week. Whenever you can, come: Point Lobos has been lauded as the greatest meeting of land and sea in the world, and crowded or not it's definitely a place you'll want to see. Point Lobos has endless vistas up and down the rocky coast, and if you don't mind a short hike, there are a number of magical beaches hidden away at its southern end.

Garrapata State Park

The northern stretches of Big Sur are marked by the rugged coves, redwood forests, and sandy beach at **Garrapata State Park,** four miles south of Point Lobos. Though it's just minutes from Carmel, Garrapata could be light-years away from the crowds of shoppers and gallery-goers, but the two-mile-long beach here is pristine and easy to reach, yet generally empty. Winter wildlife-watchers sometimes see gray whales migrating close to shore. If you really want to stretch your legs, try the seven-mile Rocky Ridge Trail through **Soberanes Canyon,** which includes a steep descent (25 percent grade!) and heads east from Hwy-1 into a lush world of redwood groves, springtime wildflowers, seasonal streams, and amazing views.

The highway clings to the coast for a dozen amazing but uneventful miles, passing a few languid cattle and an occasional vacation home before coming upon one of Big Sur's many unique sights, the massive volcanic hump of **Point Sur,** 19 miles south of Carmel. Though it's not exactly scenic or beautiful, it definitely helps you keep your bearings. A symmetrical, 361-foot dome, Point Sur is capped by a 120-year-old **lighthouse** (831/625-4419, tours Wed. and Sat.-Sun. Sept.-June, Wed.-Thurs. and Sat.-Sun. July-Aug., $12 adults), which has been preserved as a state historic park.

Andrew Molera State Park

Spreading along the coast at the mouth of the Big Sur River, 20 miles south of Carmel, **Andrew Molera State Park** is a grassy former cattle ranch on the site of one of Big Sur's oldest homesteads. In the 1850s, immigrant Juan Bautista Roger Cooper bought the land; in 1861, he built a cabin, which still stands along Hwy-1 near the park entrance. Well-blazed but sometimes boggy trails wind along both banks of the river down to the small beach, **horses** (831/625-5486) are available for hire, and there are quite a few nice places to camp (walk-in only). In winter, the park is also a popular resting spot for migrating monarch butterflies.

Big Sur Village

South of Andrew Molera, Hwy-1 cuts inland toward the heart of Big Sur, the deep and densely forested valley carved by the Big Sur River. Consisting of little more than three gas stations, a couple of roadside markets, and a number of lodges and restaurants, the mile-long village of **Big Sur** (pop. 950) represents the only real settlement between Carmel and Hearst Castle.

At the north end of town, the **Big Sur River Inn** (831/667-2700, $140 and up) has a woodsy, warm, and unpretentious restaurant overlooking the river, and rooms upstairs and across the highway. Next door is a small complex that includes crafts galleries, a grocery store with burrito bar, and the homey **Maiden Publick House** (831/667-2355), which features good beers and pub grub. Continuing south, the next mile of Hwy-1 holds Big Sur's nicest group of rustic cabins and campgrounds: Besides

The photogenic **Bixby Creek Bridge,** 15 miles south of Carmel, was one of the largest concrete bridges in the world when it was built in 1932. The old coast road runs along the north bank of the creek, linking up again with Hwy-1 near Andrew Molera State Park.

a handful of quaint cabins in a quiet location, downhill from the highway and right on the riverbanks, **Ripplewood Resort** (831/667-2242) also has a friendly 1950s café on the east side of Hwy-1, serving very good breakfasts and lunches, as well as a handy gas station and general store.

At the south end of the Big Sur village, a classic 1950s motor court has been updated and restored to its original glory (now with free Wi-Fi!) as **Glen Oaks Big Sur** (831/667-2105, $225 and up).

Pfeiffer Big Sur State Park

Roughly a half mile south of Big Sur village, **Pfeiffer Big Sur State Park** is the region's main event, a 1,000-acre riverside forest that's one of the most pleasant (and popular) parks in the state. Besides offering a full range of visitor services—restaurant, lodge, riverside campground, and grocery store—the park includes one of Big Sur's best short hikes, a three-mile loop on the Valley View trail that takes in stately redwoods, a 60-foot waterfall, and a grand vista down the Big Sur valley to the coast. The park also has the main **ranger station** (831/667-2315) for all the state parks in the Big Sur area. Just south of the park entrance, a USFS **ranger station** (831/667-2423) on the east side of Hwy-1 has information on hiking and camping opportunities in the mountains above Big Sur, including the isolated (but poison oak-ridden) **Ventana Wilderness.**

Pfeiffer Beach

South of Pfeiffer Big Sur State Park, halfway up a long, steep incline, a small road turns west and leads down through dark and heavily overgrown Sycamore Canyon, eventually winding up at Big Sur's best beach, **Pfeiffer Beach.** From the lot at the end of the road, a short trail runs through a grove of trees before opening onto the broad white sands, loomed over by a pair of hulking offshore rocks. The water's way too cold for swimming, but the half-mile strand is one of the few places in Big Sur where you can enjoy extended beachcombing strolls. The beach's northern half attracts a clothing-optional crew, even on cool, gray days.

Back along Hwy-1, just south of the turnoff for Sycamore Canyon and Pfeiffer Beach, the excellent **Big Sur Bakery & Restaurant** (831/667-0520) makes its own fresh breads and pastries, brews a rich cup of coffee, and also serves full meals—soups, steaks, and wood-fired pizzas.

Ventana Inn & Spa and the Post Ranch Inn

South of Sycamore Canyon, roughly three miles from the heart of Big Sur village, Hwy-1 passes between two of California's most deluxe small resorts. The larger of the two, **Ventana Inn & Spa** (831/667-2331 or 800/628-6500, $470 and up), covers 243 acres of Big Sur foothills and offers saunas, swimming pools, and four-star accommodations in 1970s-style cedar-paneled rooms and cabins. There's also a very fine restaurant, with incredible views and reasonable prices, to which guests are ferried in a fleet of electric carts.

Completed in 1992 and directly across Hwy-1 from Ventana, the **Post Ranch Inn** (831/667-2200 or 888/524-4787, $700 and up), a low-impact but ultra-high-style luxury resort hanging high above the Big Sur coast, is at the forefront of luxury ecotourism. In order to preserve Big Sur's untarnished natural beauty, the Post Ranch Inn is designed to be virtually invisible from land or sea. The 39 guest rooms and one private house—all featuring a king-size bed and a whirlpool bath with built-in massage table—blend in with the landscape, disguised either as playful tree houses raised up in the branches of the oaks and pines or as underground cabins carved into the cliff top. The Post Ranch restaurant, Sierra Mar, is also excellent. If you just want to have a look and plan for a future escape, free tours of the resort are given Monday-Friday at 2pm during the off-season.

Nepenthe

One of the most popular and long-lived stopping points along the Big Sur coast, **Nepenthe** (831/667-2345) is a rustic bar and restaurant offering good food and great views from atop a rocky headland some thousand feet above the Pacific. Named for the mythical drug that causes one to forget all sorrows, Nepenthe looks like something out of a 1960s James Bond movie, built of huge boulders and walls of plate glass. The food is plenty good—burgers, steaks, and fish dominate the menu—but it's the view you come here for.

Sharing a parking lot, and taking advantage of similar views, the neighboring **Cafe Kevah** (831/667-2344) serves brunch all day, plus good teas and coffees and microbrews on a rooftop deck. You'll find a gift shop downstairs selling top-quality arts and crafts and knitwear by Kaffe Fassett, whose family owns the place.

The landmark red farmhouse along Hwy-1 at the entrance to Ventana was built in 1877 by pioneer rancher W. B. Post, whose descendants developed the Post Ranch Inn.

Thirty years ago, the mighty California condor was all but extinct in the wild. Now, thanks to a successful captive breeding and reintroduction program, these massive birds can be seen soaring over the Ventana Wilderness that rises above Big Sur.

Right along Hwy-1, at a sharp bend in the road just south of Nepenthe, **The Henry Miller Memorial Library** (831/667-2574, daily) carries an erratic but engaging collection of books by and about the author, who lived in Big Sur for many years in the 1950s.

A half mile south of Nepenthe on the east side of the highway, one of the oldest and most atmospheric places to stay is **Deetjen's Big Sur Inn** (831/667-2377, $110 and up), a rambling and rustic redwood lodge built by a Norwegian immigrant in the 1930s and now a nonprofit, preservationist operation. Though the rooms are not available to families with young children unless you reserve both rooms of a two-room building, Deetjen's also serves Big Sur's best breakfasts and hearty dinners, at which all are welcome.

Julia Pfeiffer Burns State Park

If for some untenable reason you only have time to stop once along the Big Sur coast, **Julia Pfeiffer Burns State Park** (daily dawn-dusk) should be the place. Spreading along both sides of Hwy-1, about 14 miles south of Big Sur village, the park includes one truly beautiful sight: a slender waterfall that drops crisply down into a

Julia Pfeiffer Burns was a Big Sur pioneer whose family lived near Pfeiffer Beach and homesteaded much of this rugged, isolated area. In 1915, she married John Burns, a Scottish orphan who lived with the nearby Post family, and they continued to live and ranch at what is now Julia Pfeiffer Burns State Park until Julia's death in 1928.

nearly circular turquoise-blue cove. This is the only major waterfall in California that plunges directly into the Pacific.

From the parking area, east of the highway, a short trail leads under the road to a fine view of the waterfall, while another leads to the remnants of a pioneer mill, complete with a preserved Pelton wheel. Other routes climb through redwood groves up to the chaparral-covered slopes of the Santa Lucia Mountains.

About six miles south of Nepenthe, or a mile north of the parking area at Julia Pfeiffer Burns State Park, a steep fire road drops down to **Partington Cove,** where ships used to moor in the protected anchorage. The last stretch of the route passes through a 60-foot-long tunnel hewn out of solid rock.

Esalen and Lucia

Three miles south of Julia Pfeiffer Burns State Park, the New Age **Esalen Institute** (888/837-2536) takes its name from the native Esselen Indian tribe who were wiped out by European colonizers. Founded in the early 1960s by free-thinking Stanford University graduates inspired by countercultural pioneers like Gregory Bateson and Alan Watts, and set on a breathtaking cliff-top site overlooking a 180-degree coastal panorama, Esalen offers a variety of religious, philosophical, and psychological workshops, but most visitors are drawn to its incredible set of natural **hot springs** (open to the public 1pm-3am), right above the ocean. Call for information on overnight "personal retreats," or to make reservations for massages or the hot tubs.

The southern reaches of the Big Sur coast are drier and more rugged, offering bigger vistas but fewer stopping places than the northern half. The road winds along the cliffs, slowing down every 10 miles or so for each of three gas station/café/motel complexes, which pass for towns on the otherwise uninhabited coast. The northernmost of these, 9 miles south of Esalen and 25 miles south of Big Sur village, is **Lucia Lodge** (831/667-2718, $150 and up), which has wonderful ocean views, a small restaurant, and 10 creaky cabins.

High on a hill just south of Lucia, marked by a slender black cross, is the Benedictine **New Camaldoli Hermitage** (831/667-2456, around $120 a night), open to interested outsiders as a silent retreat. Rates include private rooms and veggie meals. The mix of contemplative solitude and natural beauty is hard to beat.

Nacimiento-Fergusson Road

Five miles south of Lucia, the narrow **Nacimiento-Fergusson Road** makes an unforgettable climb up from Hwy-1 over the coastal mountains. Though ravaged in places by wildfires, it's a beautiful drive, winding through hillside chaparral and dense oak groves before ending up near King City in the Salinas Valley. One real highlight here is **Mission San Antonio de Padua** (831/385-4478, daily 10am-4pm, call to confirm), a well-preserved church and monastery that is still in use by a Catholic religious community. Because the road passes through sections of Fort Hunter Liggett Army Base, you may need to show valid car registration and proof of insurance. History note: All the land on which the army base and mission stand belonged at one time to mining magnate George Hearst, whose land stretched from here all the way south and west to the coast at San Simeon, where his only child William Randolph Hearst later constructed Hearst Castle.

Near the foot of the Nacimiento-Fergusson Road is one of the few oceanside campsites in Big Sur, and perhaps the most amaz-

The roadside along Hwy-1 in the southern half of Big Sur has been invaded by thick bunches of pampas grass that crowd out local flora.

ing place to wake up on the West Coast: **Kirk Creek Campground** (805/434-1996), operated by the U.S. Forest Service. The setting is unforgettable, but so are the dastardly raccoons who are fearless in their efforts to eat your lunch before you do.

Continuing south, Hwy-1 runs past **Pacific Valley,** then passes by a number of small but pretty beaches and coves before reaching **Gorda,** the southernmost stop on the Big Sur coast. Just north of Gorda, tucked away on a knoll just east of the highway, **Treebones Resort** (877/424-4787, $215 and up) offers amazing views from its highly-rated sushi bar, plus rustic yurts and a swimming pool, all in a spectacular setting.

San Simeon: Hearst Castle

At the south end of Big Sur, the mountains flatten out and turn inland, and the coastline becomes rolling, open-range ranch land. High on a hill above Hwy-1 stands the coast's one totally unique attraction, **Hearst Castle.**

Located 65 miles south of Big Sur village and 43 miles northwest of San Luis Obispo, Hearst Castle is the sort of place that you really have to see to believe, though simple numbers—115 rooms, including 38 bedrooms in the main house alone—do give a sense of its scale.

Even if Hearst's taste in interior design (or his megalomania, which by all accounts was understated in his fictional portrayal in Orson Welles's *Citizen Kane*) doesn't appeal, Hearst Castle cries out to be seen. One of the last century's most powerful and influential Americans (the Rupert Murdoch of his day), Hearst inherited the land, and most of his fortune, from his mother, Phoebe Apperson Hearst (his father was George Hearst, a mining mogul), and began work on his castle following the death of his mother in 1919. With the help of the great California architect Julia Morgan, who designed the complex to look like a Mediterranean hill town with Hearst's house as the cathedral at its center, Hearst spent more than 25 years working on his "castle"—building, rebuilding, and filling room after room with furniture—all the while entertaining the great and powerful of the era, from Charlie Chaplin to Winston Churchill.

A small **museum** (daily, free) in the visitors center, next to where you board the trams that carry you up to the house, details Hearst's life and times. If you want to go on a **tour** (800/444-4445, $25 and up adults), the Grand Rooms Tour gives the best first-time overview, taking in a few

William Randolph Hearst

rooms of the main house. There's also an Upstairs Suites Tour and a Cottages & Kitchen Tour; each takes around 45 minutes, not including transit time. All tours also come with the option of watching a 40-minute movie giving the background on Hearst and his house-building. Advance reservations are all but essential, especially in summer.

Since Hearst Castle is rather isolated, it's a good idea to stay the night before or after a visit at nearby **San Simeon,** which has grown into a massive strip of motels. There's a pair of inexpensive overnight options: the **San Simeon Lodge** (9520 Castillo Dr., 805/927-4601, $60 and up) or **Motel 6.**

At Piedras Blancas, just north of Hearst Castle, the roadside along Hwy-1 has been taken over by herds of massive, bellowing elephant seals, a once-threatened but clearly resurgent species of massive pinnipeds who congregate here every winter to fight and procreate.

Cambria

Without Hearst Castle, **Cambria** would be just another farming town, but being next to one of the state's top tourist attractions has turned Cambria into quite a busy little hive. Apart from a few hokey, tourist-trapping souvenir shops at the north end of town, it's a casual, walkable, and franchise-free community of arts and crafts galleries, boutiques, and good restaurants; from Hwy-1, Main Street makes a three-mile loop around to the east, running through the heart of town.

Hearty breakfasts are available at the **Redwood Cafe** (2094 Main St., 805/927-4830), while well-prepared multi-ethnic and vegetarian food is on the menu at **Robin's** (4095 Burton Dr., 805/927-5007), a half block off Main Street. For barbecue, burgers, and beer, check out the **Main Street Grill** (603 Main St.,

805/927-3194, cash only). Places to stay range from nice, older motels like the **Bluebird Inn** (1880 Main St., 800/552-5434, $68 and up) to the spacious suites and cabins at **Cambria Pines Lodge** (2905 Burton Dr., 805/927-4200, $89 and up), which has a nice pool high on a hill between town and the beach. For a relaxing overnight, try the lovely little **Bridge Street Inn** (4314 Bridge St., 805/927-7653), a block from downtown, which offers very reasonable B&B rooms as well as shared HI-approved hostel beds.

Five miles south of Cambria, **Harmony** (pop. 18) is a former dairy town turned arts and crafts colony, with a range of galleries and a small wedding chapel.

Cayucos

Though it doesn't really look like much from Hwy-1, which has grown into a near-freeway to carry all the Hearst Castle traffic, the coastal town of **Cayucos** is definitely worth a look. Sitting along the coast 15 miles south of Cambria, not far from Morro Bay, Cayucos has a nice little beach, a fishing pier, a range of surfing and skateboard shops, and at least two unusual places to eat and drink. If you like tiki-style bars, you'll want to save your thirst for a visit to **Schooners Wharf** (171 N. Ocean Ave., 805/995-3883), with good mojitos and variable food, served up in a landmark bar room downstairs, or on an oceanview terrace above. For great food at fair prices, don't miss **Ruddell's Smokehouse** (101 D St., 805/995-5028), just off the beach, where the no-frills menu features smoked salmon and tuna sandwiches, plus fish, pork, and chicken tacos.

Morro Bay

Marked by the Gibraltar-like monolith of Morro Rock, which was noted by Juan Rodriguez Cabrillo in 1542 and now serves as a peregrine falcon preserve and nesting site, **Morro Bay** (pop. 10,436) surrounds a busy commercial fishing harbor a half mile west of Hwy-1. A thin, three-mile-long strip of sand protects the bay from the Pacific Ocean, forming a seabird-rich lagoon that's included within **Morro Bay State Park,** a mile southeast of Morro Rock. There's an excellent **museum** ($3 adults) with displays on local wildlife, and the park also contains the friendly **Bayside Cafe** (805/772-1465), serving lunch and dinner. Next door, when the weather's nice, you can rent **kayaks** (805/772-8796) and paddle around the estuary.

The James Dean Memorial, 27 miles east of Paso Robles near the junction of Highways 46 and 41, is a stark, stainless-steel sculpture near the site where the talented and rebellious actor crashed in his silver Porsche and died on September 30, 1955. The highway has also been signed in Dean's memory.

The rest of Morro Bay is pretty quiet; one unusual sight is a giant **outdoor chessboard** (with waist-high playing pieces) at the foot of Morro Bay Boulevard on the waterfront in City Park. For clam chowder or fish-and-chips, try **Giovanni's** (1001 Front St., 805/772-2123) in the strollable waterfront neighborhood. Very good, fast, Mexican-themed "fusion" food is available at the **Taco Temple** (2680 Main St., 805/772-4965), an often crowded and grandly named fish shack on the land side of the Hwy-1 frontage, a mile north of town.

San Luis Obispo

Located midway between San Francisco and Los Angeles at the junction of Hwy-1 and US-101, **San Luis Obispo** (pop. 44,174) makes a good stopping-off point, at least for lunch if not for a lengthier stay. Like most of the towns along this route, San Luis, as it's almost always called, revolves around an 18th-century mission, here named **Mission San Luis Obispo de Tolosa.** Standing at the heart of town, at Chorro and Monterey Streets, the mission overlooks one of the state's liveliest small-town downtown districts, with dozens of shops and restaurants backing onto **Mission Plaza,** a two-block park on the banks of Mission Creek.

Besides the mission and the lively downtown commercial district that surrounds it, not to mention the nearly 20,000 students buzzing around the nearby campus of Cal Poly San Luis Obispo, San Luis holds a singular roadside attraction, the **Madonna Inn** (805/543-3000 or 800/543-9666, $170 and up), which stands just west of US-101 at the foot of town. One of California's most noteworthy pop culture landmarks, the Madonna Inn is a remarkable example of what architecturally minded academic types like to call vernacular kitsch. Created by local contractor Alex Madonna, who died in 2004, the Madonna Inn offers 100 unique rooms,

each decorated in a wild barrage of fantasy motifs: There's a bright pink honeymoon suite known as "Love Nest," the "Safari" room covered in fake zebra skins with a jungle-green carpet, and the cave-like "Caveman" Room. *Roadside America* rates it as "the best place to spend a vacation night in America," but even if you can't stay, at least stop for a look at the gift shop, which sells postcards of the different rooms. Guys should head down to the men's room, where the urinal trough is flushed by a waterfall.

Though the Madonna Inn has a huge, banquet-ready restaurant—done up in white lace and varying hues of pink—the best places to eat are downtown, near the mission. **Linnaea's Cafe** (1110 Garden St., 805/541-5888), off Higuera, serves coffee and tea and sundry snack items all day and night; there's also the lively, veggie-friendly **Big Sky Cafe** (1121 Broad St., 805/545-5401) and the usual range of beer-and-burger bars you'd expect from a college town. For something very special, the heart of SLO holds one of the central coast's great restaurants, **Novo** (726 Higuera St., 805/543-3986), serving locally sourced and very fresh Mediterranean-inspired meals on a nice terrace backing onto Mission Plaza. Great bar, too.

The world's first motel opened in 1925 at 2223 Monterey Street, San Luis Obispo. Originally called the Milestone Mo-Tel, the Spanish revival structure was later renamed the Motel Inn, but it went out of business long ago, and its remnants now stand next to US-101 on the grounds of the Apple Farm restaurant and motel.

Along with the Madonna Inn, San Luis has a number of good places to stay, with reasonable rates that drop considerably after the summertime peak season. Besides the national chains, try the **Peach Tree Inn** (2001 Monterey St., 800/227-6396, $89 and up) or **La Cuesta Inn** (2074 Monterey St., 800/543-2777, $189 and up). There's also the **HI-Hostel Obispo** (1617 Santa Rosa St., 805/544-4678), with 28 beds in a converted Victorian cottage near downtown and the Amtrak station.

Pismo Beach

South of San Luis Obispo, Hwy-1 and US-101 run along the ocean past **Pismo Beach** (pop. 7,655), a family-oriented beach resort where the main attraction is driving or dune-buggying along the sands. Pismo was once famous for its clams, now over-harvested to the point of oblivion. While you may still see people pitchforking a few small ones out of the surf, you won't find any on local menus. Like the rest of Southern California, the Pismo area has grown significantly in the past two decades, thanks mainly to an influx of retired people housed in red-roofed townhouses. Price Street, the old main road running through the heart of the old small town, still offers a wide range of motels and restaurants, like the very popular **Cracked Crab** (751 Price St., 805/773-2722), which has fish-and-chips and a crazy range of fresh crab and other crustaceans (almost all of which come from Alaska). For a close approximation of Pismo's once-abundant clams, walk two blocks from the Cracked Crab, past the bowling alley, to another seafood specialist, the **Splash Café** (197 Pomeroy Ave., 805/773-4653), which is locally famous for clam chowder served up in edible bowls made of freshly baked bread.

While Pismo is most popular for summer fun, every winter a grove of trees just south of downtown turns into a prime gathering spot for migrating monarch butterflies. The largest groupings, numbering in the tens of thou-

A pedestrian walkway in downtown San Luis Obispo, off Higuera Street between Garden and Broad Streets, has become known around the world as **Bubblegum Alley.** Since the 1950s, local kids have written their names and allegiances on the brick walls, using chewing gum rather than the more contemporary spray paint.

Every Thursday evening, the main drag of San Luis Obispo, **Higuera Street,** is closed to cars and converted into a very lively farmers market and block party, with stands selling fresh food and good live bands providing entertainment.

EL CAMINO REAL AND
THE CALIFORNIA MISSIONS

While the American colonies were busy rebelling against the English Crown, a handful of Spaniards and Mexicans were establishing outposts and blazing an overland route up the California coast, along the New World's most distant frontier. Beginning in 1769 with the founding of a fortress and a Franciscan mission at San Diego, and culminating in 1823 with the founding of another outpost at what is now San Francisco, a series of small but self-reliant religious colonies was established, each a day's travel apart and linked by El Camino Real, The King's Highway, a route followed roughly by today's US-101.

Some of the most interesting missions are listed here, north to south, followed by the dates of their founding.

San Francisco Solano (1823). The only mission built under Mexican rule stands at the heart of Sonoma, a history-rich Wine Country town.

San Juan Bautista (1797). This lovely church forms the heart of an extensive historic park, in the town of the same name (see page 89).

San Carlos Borroméo de Carmelo (1771). Also known as **Carmel Mission,** this was the most important of the California missions (see page 95).

San Antonio de Padua (1771). This reconstructed church, still in use as a monastery, stands in an undeveloped valley inland from Big Sur in the middle of Fort Hunter Liggett Army training center. Monks still live, work, and pray here, making for a marvelously evocative visit (see page 103).

Mission San Fernando from Memory Garden, and Father Junípero Serra Statue

San Miguel Arcángel (1797). This is the only mission not to have undergone extensive renovations and restorations—almost everything, notably the vibrantly colorful interior murals, is as it was.

La Purisima Mission (1787). A quiet coastal valley is home to this church, which was restored in the 1930s using traditional methods as part of a New Deal employment and training project (see page 113).

Santa Barbara (1786). Called the Queen of the Missions, this lovely church stands in lush gardens above the upscale coastal city (see page 116).

San Gabriel Arcángel (1771). Once the most prosperous of the California missions, it now stands quietly and all but forgotten off a remnant of Route 66 east of Los Angeles.

San Juan Capistrano (1776). Known for the swallows that return here each year, this mission has lovely gardens (see page 131).

© AVALON TRAVEL

At the south end of Pismo Beach, beyond the scruffy farmlands that surround the wide mouth of the Santa Maria River, **Guadalupe-Nipomo Dunes National Wildlife Refuge** holds endless acres of windswept beaches, coastal sand dunes, and boggy bird-friendly marshlands, as well as the buried remains of a movie set used in Cecil B. DeMille's *The Ten Commandments.*

In 1936, **Nipomo** was the place where Dorothea Lange took that famous photograph of a migrant mother huddling with her children in a farm-worker camp.

sands, though decreasing disturbingly quickly in recent years, are usually found roosting at the North Beach Campground of Pismo State Beach, along Hwy-1 off Dolliver Street.

Guadalupe and Santa Maria

South of Pismo Beach, California's coastal highways again diverge. Hwy-1 cuts off west through the still-agricultural areas around sleepy **Guadalupe** (pop. 6,296), where produce stands sell cabbages, broccoli, and leafy green vegetables fresh from the fields. The town itself feels miles away from modern California, with a four-block Main Street lined by Mexican cafés, bars, banks, and grocery stores.

If you opt to follow US-101, shopping malls and tract-house suburbs fill the inland valleys through rapidly suburbanizing **Santa Maria.** Among barbecue aficionados, the Santa Maria region is famous for its thick cuts of salsa-slathered barbecued beef, which can best be sampled at **Jocko's** (125 N. Thompson Ave., 805/929-3565, Mon.-Sat. from 4:30pm, Sun. from 1pm) in **Nipomo,** east of US-101 at the Tefft Street exit. Great steaks (and mouthwateringly moist, inch-thick barbecued pork chops!) highlight the no-frills Jocko's menu, which is cooked over oak charcoal.

Lompoc and La Purisima Mission

The rolling valleys around **Lompoc** are famed for their production of flower seeds, and consequently the fields along Hwy-1 are often ablaze in brilliant colors. Apart from colorful murals adorning downtown buildings, Lompoc as a town is not up to much, despite the unusual nature of the area's two main nonagricultural employers. One is a minimum-security federal prison; the other is Vandenberg Air Force Base, site of numerous missile tests, the aborted West Coast space shuttle port, and the $60 billion "Son of Star Wars" National Missile Defense program.

With its long arcade reaching across the floor of a shallow,

Lompoc flower fields

grassy valley, **La Purisima Mission** (805/733-3713, daily, $6 per car) gives a strong first impression of what the missions may have looked like in their prime. Four miles northeast of Lompoc, between Hwy-1 and US-101 on Hwy-246, the mission here was originally built in 1812 but fell to ruin before being totally reconstructed as part of a WPA make-work scheme in the New Deal 1930s. During the restoration, workers used period techniques wherever possible, hewing logs with hand tools and stomping mud and straw with their bare feet to mix it for adobe bricks. Workers also built most of the mission-style furniture that fills the chapel and the other rooms in the complex. Other features include a functioning aqueduct, many miles of hiking trails, and a small museum.

Buellton and Solvang

The town of **Buellton,** a block west of US-101 at the Solvang exit, holds one of California's classic roadside landmarks, **Pea Soup Andersen's** (376 Ave. of the Flags, 805/688-5581), advertised up and down the coast. Another Buellton landmark, **The Hitching Post II** (406 E. Mission Dr., 805/688-0676), a little ways east of US-101, starred in the wine-loving road-trip movie *Sideways.*

Four miles east of Buellton and US-101, America's most famous mock-European tourist trap, the Danish-style town of **Solvang** (pop. 5,245), was founded in 1911. Set up by a group of Danish immigrants as a cooperative agricultural community, Solvang found its calling catering to passing travelers. The compact blocks of cobblestone streets and Old World architecture, highlighted by a few windmills and signs advertising the Hamlet Inn among many more suspicious claims to Danishness, now attract tourists

The late great pop singer Michael Jackson's **Neverland Ranch** lies here in the foothills of the Santa Ynez Valley, southeast of Solvang via the truly scenic Hwy-154, which loops inland south to Santa Barbara, arriving via a steep and stunning drive over San Marcos Pass.

Rancho del Cielo, the ranch of former President Ronald Reagan, spreads along the crest of the coastal hills above Refugio State Beach.

by the busload. Many other U.S. towns (Leavenworth, Washington, and Helen, Georgia, to name two) have been inspired by Solvang's success, but to be honest there's nothing much to do here apart from walking, gawking, and shopping for pastries.

Just east of Solvang's windmills and gables, the brooding hulk of **Old Mission Santa Inés** stands as a sober reminder of the region's Spanish colonial past. Built in 1804, it was once among the more prosperous of the California missions but now is worth a visit mainly for the gift shop selling all manner of devotional ornaments.

Gaviota State Park and Refugio State Beach

Between Solvang and Santa Barbara, US-101 follows the coast past some of California's most beautiful beaches. Dropping through a steep-sided canyon, US-101 reaches the coast at **Gaviota State Park,** where a small fishing pier and campground are overwhelmed by the massive train trestle that runs overhead. Continuing south, US-101 runs atop coastal bluffs past prime surfing beaches, usually marked by a few VWs pulled out along the west side of the highway. Midway along this stretch of coast, some 22 miles north of Santa Barbara, **Refugio State Beach** has groves of palm trees backing a clear white strand. There's also a small, summer-only store, and a number of attractive campsites with hot showers. Reservations for **camping** (800/444-7275) at Gaviota or Refugio, or at any California state beach, should be made in advance.

Santa Barbara

The geographical midpoint of California may well be somewhere near San Francisco, but the Southern California of popular imagination—golden beaches washed by waves and peopled by blond-

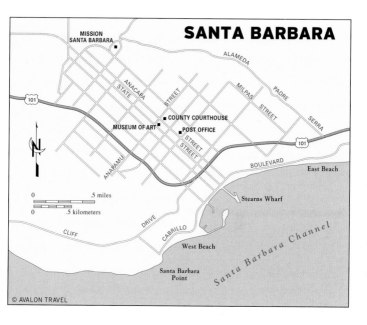

haired surfer gods—has its start, and perhaps best expression, in **Santa Barbara** (pop. 88,410). Around 100 miles north of Los Angeles, Santa Barbara has grown threefold in the last 60 years, but for the moment, at least, it manages to retain its sleepy seaside charm. Much of its character comes from the fact that, following a sizable earthquake in 1925, the town fathers—caught up in the contemporary craze for anything Spanish Revival—required that all buildings in the downtown area exude a mission-era feel, mandating red-tile roofs, adobe-colored stucco, and rounded arcades wherever practicable. The resulting architectural consistency gives Santa Barbara an un-American charm; it looks more like a Mediterranean village than the modern city that, beneath the surface, it really is.

For a good first look at the city head down to the water, where **Stearns Wharf** sticks out into the bay, bordered by palm tree-lined beaches populated by joggers, in-line skaters, and volleyball players. From the wharf area, follow State Street away from the sands to the downtown district, where Santa Barbarans parade among the numerous cafés, bars, and boutiques. At the north end of downtown is the excellent **Santa Barbara Museum of Art** (1130 State St., 805/963-4364, closed Mon., $10 adults). A block east on Anacapa Street, the **County Courthouse** is one of the finest public buildings in the state, a hand-crafted Spanish Revival monument set in lush semitropical gardens, with an **observation tower** (weekdays 8am-5pm, weekends 10am-4:30pm, free) giving a fine view over the red-tiled cityscape.

Santa Barbara's reigning attraction, **Old Mission Santa Barbara** (805/682-4713, daily, $7 for self-guided tours), stands atop a shallow hill a well-posted mile up from State Street, looking out over the city and shoreline below. Called the "Queen of the Missions" by the local tourist scribes, Mission Santa Barbara is undeniably lovely to look at, its rose-hued stone facade perfectly complemented by the roses and bougainvillea that frame the well-maintained gardens and lawns.

Santa Barbara is one of many great places along the coast to go on a **whale-watching cruise** (805/963-3564 or 888/779-4253), on the *Condor Express* or other boats, to see migrating gray whales in winter and jumping humpbacks in summer. Trips take a half day or full day, and some head out to the Channel Islands; call for details or reservations.

Santa Barbara has perhaps the south coast's best variety of places to eat. State Street holds the most lunch and dinner places, like the old-fashioned burgers and beer on tap in the 1920s dark-wood dining room of **Joe's Cafe** (536 State St., 805/966-4638). Fans of grilled burgers and hot pastrami sandwiches will enjoy the tasty local chain **The Habit** (628 State St., 805/892-5400), which started in collegiate Isla Vista, near UCSB. There's excellent fresh sushi at **Arigato Sushi** (1225 State St., 805/965-6074), while some of the world's best hole-in-the-wall Mexican food is served a half mile east of State Street at **La Super-Rica** (622 N. Milpas St., 805/963-4940, closed Wed.), where such distinguished foodies as Julia Child have come to chow down on a variety of freshly made soft tacos and delicious seafood tamales. It's not cheap, but the food is great (fresh tortillas, traditional *adobado*-marinated pork, and spicy chorizo), and the *horchata* is the creamiest you'll taste. Yum.

The city's accommodations, however, are among the central coast's most expensive, especially in summer when even the most basic motel can charge as much as $200 a night. One of the nicest of many motels is **The Franciscan Inn** (109 Bath St., 805/963-8845, $145 and up), just a short walk from the beach and wharf. At the top of the scale, the **Simpson House Inn** (121 E. Arrellaga St.,

805/963-7067 or 800/676-1280, $300 and up) offers comfortable, centrally located B&B rooms. Off the scale completely, money's-no-object visitors can enjoy the deluxe facilities of the **San Ysidro Ranch** (805/565-1700, $695 and up), in the hills above neighboring **Montecito,** where Jackie and JFK spent some of their honeymoon. Somewhat ironically, considering the generally high prices here, international budget chain **Motel 6** (443 Corona Del Mar, 805/564-1392, $85 and up) got its start in Santa Barbara, where it now has five area properties, including the recently-redesigned original one near the beach.

Channel Islands National Park

South of Santa Barbara, US-101 widens into an eight-lane freeway along the coast. Looking out across the Pacific, beyond the partially disguised offshore oil wells, you can't miss seeing the sharp outlines of the **Channel Islands,** whose rocky, tide-pool-packed shores are protected as a national park. Consisting of eight islands altogether (five are part of the park), they sit from 12 to about 60 miles off the mainland. Numerous scenic cruises around the Channel

Islands start from Santa Barbara, but only the closest, **Anacapa Island,** is easily accessible to the public, via daily trips from Ventura Harbor offered by **Island Packers** (805/642-1393, $59 adults). Bring water, as none is available on the island; camping is possible, but reservations are required.

Ventura and Oxnard

Midway between Malibu and Santa Barbara, downtown **Ventura** (pop. 106,433) is an offbeat little place, its three-block Main Street lined by enough thrift shops (seven at last count) to clothe a destitute retro-minded army. Apart from searching out vintage couture, the main reason to stop is the small and much-reconstructed **Mission San Buenaventura** (211 E. Main St., daily, $4 adults), standing at the center of Ventura just north of the US-101 freeway. This was the ninth in the California mission chain, and the last one founded by Father Junípero Serra, in 1782.

Ventura doesn't get anything like the tourist trade that Santa Barbara draws, but it does have the very pleasant **Bella Maggiore**

Inn (67 S. California St., 805/652-0277 or 800/523-8479, $75 and up), offering good-value B&B rooms in a nicely restored 1920s courtyard hotel between downtown and US-101.

South of Ventura, US-101 heads inland through the San Fernando Valley to Hollywood and downtown Los Angeles, while Hwy-1 heads south through the 10 miles of stop-and-go sprawl that make up the rapidly suburbanizing farming community of **Oxnard** (pop. 197,899), then continues right along the coast through Malibu and West Los Angeles.

As an introduction to the high-style car culture of Southern California, there's no better stop than Oxnard's unexpected treasure trove, the **Mullin Automotive Museum** (1421 Emerson Ave., 805/385-5400, $15). Though it is open barely two days a month, the chance to appreciate one of the world's finest car collections may be worth planning your trip around.

> Ventura is the birthplace and headquarters of the outdoor equipment and clothing company Patagonia, started and still owned by legendary rock climber Yvon Chouinard.

Simi Valley

If you opt to follow US-101 rather than coastal Hwy-1 into Los Angeles, be sure to check out the somnolent suburb of **Simi Valley**, 30 miles east of Ventura, where the hilltop **Ronald Reagan Presidential Library** (805/522-2977, daily, $21 adults) fills 150,000 square feet of Spanish-style stucco with a fascinating array of exhibits and artifacts, most famously a chunk of the Berlin Wall, set in a Cold War-era tableau. Also here, housed in a 200-foot-long glass-walled pavilion, is the actual Boeing 707 used as presidential Air Force One by Nixon, Carter, Ford, Reagan, George H. W. Bush, Clinton, and George W. Bush. The "Great Communicator" was interred here following his death in 2004. To get to the

Tressa Prisbrey's Bottle Village

library, take US-101 to Hwy-23 North (a.k.a. the Ronald Reagan Freeway), exit at Olsen Road, and follow the signs.

The other Simi Valley sight to see is **Grandma Prisbey's Bottle Village** (4595 Cochran St., 805/231-2497, $10), a complex of small buildings and sculptures built out of glass bottles, TV sets, hubcaps, and assorted other recycled refuse. The late Tressa Prisbey started building it in 1956. Subject of an ongoing battle between folk-art preservationists and those who think it's a pile of junk, the "village" can be viewed less than a mile south of the Hwy-118/210 freeway between the Tapo Street and Stearns Street exits.

Pacific Coast Highway Beaches

Running right along the beach, the Pacific Coast Highway (Hwy-1) heads south from Oxnard around the rocky headland of **Point Mugu** (pronounced "ma-GOO"), where the U.S. Navy operates a missile testing center and the Santa Monica Mountains rise steeply out of the Pacific Ocean. Most of these chaparral-covered granite mountains have been protected as parkland, with hiking, cycling, and riding trails offering grand views and a surprising amount of solitude. Before or after a hike in the hills (or a Harley ride along the coast, the preferred mode of arrival), the ramshackle **Neptune's Net** restaurant (42505 Pacific Coast Hwy., 310/457-3095) is a great place to hang out and "star"-gaze while enjoying fresh seafood, served up on paper plates for that down-home Hollywood feel.

South from here, state-owned beaches mark your progress along the coastal road, but this stretch is basically natural wilderness—apart from the highway, of course. Biggest and best of the beaches hereabouts is the lovely **Leo Carrillo State Park** (310/457-8143), which has a sandy strand, some great tide pools, and a sycamore-shaded **campground** (reservations 800/444-7275). Leo Carrillo (1880-1961) was an actor (he played Pancho in *The Cisco Kid* TV show) and preservationist who was instrumental in expanding the California state parks.

South of Leo Carrillo, which marks the Los Angeles County line, there are many more public beach areas, including (in roughly north-to-south order) **Nicholas Canyon County Beach, El Pescador State Beach,** and **El Matador State Beach** (where episodes of TV's *Baywatch* have been filmed). At big, brash **Zuma Beach County Park,** where volleyball courts and snack bars line the sands, the PCH bends inland around the headlands of **Point Dume State Beach,** a great spot for winter whale-watching.

Malibu

South of Zuma Beach, houses begin popping up along Hwy-1 to block the oceanfront views, and more-elaborate multimillion-dollar homes dot the canyons above as well, forming the sprawling exurbia and movie-star playground of **Malibu,** which stretches along Hwy-1 for the next 27 miles into Santa Monica and metropolitan Los Angeles. Unless TV helicopters are flying overhead to document the latest wildfire or other natural disaster, it's hard to get more than a glimpse of the garage doors or wrought-iron gates of these palaces, but this is the address of choice for the movers and shakers of the entertainment world: If you can name them, they probably own property here. Most of the truly huge estates are hidden away on ranches high up in the mountains.

One of these hideaways has been evolving since 1993, when Barbra Streisand donated her 22.5-acre ranch for use as a botanical preserve. Called **Ramirez Canyon Park** (5750 Ramirez Canyon Rd.), it's managed by the Santa Monica Mountains Conservancy and is open by appointment only, thanks to requests from neighbors. Ramirez Canyon meets the Pacific at the aptly named **Paradise Cove,** a private beach and boat launch which is worth checking out for the excellent little **Paradise Cove Beach Café** (28128 Pacific Coast Hwy., 310/457-9791), serving what may well be the world's best grilled cheese sandwiches. Here they come complete with carmelized onions, spectacular ocean views, and frequent activity by

Malibu Pier at sunset

film and TV crews. *Baywatch* and *The Rockford Files* were both filmed on the sands and the rustic pier.

This stretch of coastline holds another great place to eat: **Malibu Seafood** (25653 Pacific Coast Hwy., 310/456-3430), a low-key beach shack drawing local gardeners, pool guys, and Hollywood starlets for BYOB fish-and-chips.

The main route inland from the coast, Malibu Canyon Road, was the setting of the key murder scene in James M. Cain's thriller ***The Postman Always Rings Twice.***

Continuing south along high-speed Hwy-1, the most prominent sight is the **Pepperdine University** campus, which was described by the late, great architect Charles Moore as "an overscaled motel set in obscenely vivid emerald lawns." Below the bluff-top campus, the legendary **Malibu Colony** of celebrity homes stretches along the coast in high-security splendor. Just north of Pepperdine, a short drive up Corral Canyon Road gives access to Solstice Canyon, part of the **Santa Monica Mountains National Recreation Area,** where a well-marked, mile-long hiking trail leads through scrubby native chaparral up to a delicate spring waterfall, past numerous signs of the frequent fall wildfires (like the 4,900-acre Corral Fire of November 2007, which destroyed Malibu's oldest home; the remains are preserved in situ).

Away from the mountains, about the only place in Malibu proper where it's fun (and legal) to explore is the area around the landmark **Malibu Pier,** which juts into the ocean at the heart of Malibu's short and rather scruffy commercial strip. North of the pier stretches **Surfrider Beach,** site of most of those Frankie Avalon and Annette Funicello *Beach Blanket Bingo*-type movies made during the 1950s. The pier and the beach are part of **Malibu Lagoon State Beach,** which also protects the historic **Adamson House** (23200 Pacific Coast Hwy., 310/456-8432, Wed.-Sat. 11am-3pm, $7 adults), a lovely circa-1930 Spanish Revival courtyard home, right on the beach and full of gorgeous tile work and other architectural features. Tours of the house are given throughout the day, and fascinating exhibits portray Malibu history and the Rindge family, who once owned the entire region.

Topanga and the Getty Villa

Between Malibu and Santa Monica, **Topanga Canyon** is one of the last great wild spaces in Los Angeles, with a number of parks, trails, and perhaps the last wild and free waterways—steelhead trout still spawn in the waters of Topanga Creek, which flows down from the mountains to the Santa Monica Bay. Home to an alternative-minded community of some 8,000 hippies and New Agers (Neil Young recorded *After the Gold Rush* in his home here), Topanga was first established as an artists' colony in the 1950s by the likes of Woody Guthrie and actor Will Geer, who played Grandpa in TV's *The Waltons,* long after he'd been blacklisted during the anti-Communist McCarthy witch hunts. For the past 30 years Geer's old property has been preserved as the **Theatricum Botanicum** (1419 N. Topanga Canyon Blvd., 310/455-2322), a garden and politically minded 300-seat open-air theater, six miles up the canyon.

South of Topanga, and once again open to the public after a nearly 10-year, $275-million remodeling, are the world-famous antiquities of **The J. Paul Getty Museum** (310/440-7300, closed Tues., free, $15 per car, good at both museum sites). Over 1,200 priceless classics are displayed in the pseudo-Pompeiian Getty Villa, where the oil magnate's art collection was housed prior to the construction of the massive Getty Center complex along the I-405 freeway above Brentwood. Admission to the Getty Villa is free, but parking reservations are essential.

From the Getty Villa south to Santa Monica, the Pacific Coast Highway (Hwy-1) runs along the wide-open sands of **Will Rogers State Beach,** gifted to the public by the Depression-era humorist.

Crossing Los Angeles

From Malibu and Topanga Canyon, Hwy-1 swoops along the shore, running along the beach as far as the landmark Santa Monica Pier before bending inland through a tunnel and metamorphosing quite unexpectedly into the I-10 Santa Monica Freeway. The second exit off this freeway (which has been officially dubbed the Christopher Columbus Transcontinental Highway, running all the way east to Jacksonville, Florida) takes you to Lincoln Boulevard, which carries the Hwy-1 moniker south through Venice and Marina del Rey to Los Angeles International Airport (LAX), where it runs into Sepulveda Boulevard.

After passing through a tunnel under the airport runways—worth

the drive just for the experience of seeing 747s taxiing over your head—Sepulveda emerges in the Tarantino-esque communities of L.A.'s "South Bay," which utterly lack the glamour of chichi Santa Monica and Malibu. At Hermosa Beach, one of a trio of pleasant if surprisingly blue-collar beach towns, Sepulveda Boulevard changes its name to Pacific Coast Highway, then bends inland to bypass the ritzy communities of the Palos Verdes Peninsula, passing instead through the industrial precincts of San Pedro that border the Los Angeles/Long Beach harbor, one of the busiest on the West Coast.

Since Hwy-1 follows slow-moving Lincoln Boulevard and other surface streets across L.A., if you are in any sort of hurry you should stay on the Santa Monica Freeway (I-10) east to the San Diego Freeway (I-405), and follow that south as far as you're going. Coming from the south, follow these freeways in reverse order—or risk the time-consuming consequences.

Long Beach

Directly south of downtown Los Angeles, the city of **Long Beach** (pop. 462,257) is the second-largest of L.A.'s constituent cities, but it feels more like the Midwest than the cutting-edge West Coast. Long Beach is probably best known as the home of the cruise ship RMS Queen Mary (877/342-0738, tours $25.95), one of the largest and most luxurious liners ever to set sail. Impossible to miss as it looms over Long Beach harbor, the stately ship is open for self-guided tours. You can also stay overnight in one of the many staterooms and cabins, traveling back to a more elegant time for surprisingly reasonable overnight rates. In place of Howard Hughes's famous "Spruce Goose" airplane, which used to stand next door, there's now a Cold War-era submarine.

Across the bay on the main downtown Long Beach waterfront, the **Aquarium of the Pacific** (562/590-3100, daily, $30 adults) explores the diverse ecosystems of the Pacific Ocean, from tropical coral reefs (shown off in an amazing, 350,000-gallon display) to the frigid waters of the Bering Sea. The tanks full of jellyfish of all kinds, colors, and sizes are the main event.

Other Long Beach attractions include the **"World's Largest Mural,"** a 115,000-square-foot painting of migrating gray whales on the outside of the Long Beach Arena, and the self-proclaimed **"Skinniest House in the USA"** (708 Gladys Ave.).

Long Beach also marks the southern end of L.A.'s reborn streetcar and subway system, and you can ride the Blue Line north to downtown and connect to everywhere else. It's an inexpensive base for exploring the Los Angeles area, especially if you avail yourself of the **HI-Los Angeles South Bay Hostel** (3601 S. Gaffey St., 310/831-8109), in a peaceful locale on a hill overlooking the harbor area. There's also a **Best Western** (1725 Long Beach Blvd., 562/599-5555, $96 and up) directly across from a Blue Line train stop.

Los Angeles

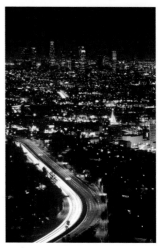

the Los Angeles skyline, as seen from Mulholland Drive

Love it or hate it, one thing you can't do about L.A. is ignore it. Thanks to Hollywood in all its many guises (movies, television, the music industry), the city is always in the headlines. Without falling too deeply under the spell of its hyperbole-fueled image-making machinery, it's safe to say that L.A. definitely has something for everyone. In keeping with its car-centered culture, however, our suggested tour ignores the many individual attractions and focuses instead on a pair of quintessential L.A. drives.

Winding along the crest of the Hollywood Hills, **Mulholland Drive** is the classic L.A. cruise. Starting in the east within sight of the Hollywood sign and the Hollywood Bowl, this ribbon of two-lane blacktop passes by the city's most valuable real estate, giving great views on both sides, both by day and after dark.

Another classic L.A. cruise, running from the scruffy fringes of downtown all the way west to the coast, **Sunset Boulevard** gives glimpses into almost every conceivable aspect of Los Angeles life. Starting downtown, the historic core of colonial Los Angeles and now a showcase of contemporary architecture thanks to a stunning new cathedral and concert hall, Sunset Boulevard's 27-mile course then winds west past Echo Park and Hollywood to West Hollywood, where it becomes the Sunset Strip, still the liveliest nightclub district in town. Continuing west, Sunset winds through Beverly Hills, Brentwood, and Bel-Air, lined by the largest mansions you're likely to see, before ending up at the edge of the Pacific Ocean.

The **Los Angeles Dodgers** (866/363-4377) play at beautiful Dodger Stadium, on a hill above downtown.

PRACTICALITIES

Most flights into Los Angeles arrive at Los Angeles International Airport (LAX), on the coast southwest of downtown, where you'll find all the usual shuttles and rental car agencies. Other useful L.A.-area airports include Bob Hope (BUR) in Burbank and John Wayne (SNA) in Orange County.

Before choosing a place to stay, think about where you want to spend your time and settle near there. High-end places abound, but character can be hard to come by. Along the coast, recommended accommodations range from the handy **HI-Santa Monica Hostel** (1436 2nd St., 310/393-9913, starts at $32 per person), a block from the beach, to the unique *Queen Mary* (877/342-0738, $89 and up) in Long Beach, a hotel offering authentic art deco-era staterooms in the fabulous old luxury liner. Midrange with a great mid-city location, try the **Farmer's Daughter Hotel** (115 S. Fairfax Ave., 323/937-3930, $199 and up), next to the historic Farmers Market, a very friendly 1950s-style motel with tons of charm and the city's hottest new shopping mall and entertainment complex, The Grove, across the street. Downtown, the most fabulous place to stay is the retro-1960s **The Standard, Downtown LA** (550 S. Flower St., 213/892-8080, $216 and up), with the world's coolest rooftop, poolside bar.

For food, one place I always try to stop is **The Apple Pan** (10801 W. Pico Blvd., 310/475-3585), an ancient (circa-1947) landmark on the West L.A. landscape, serving the best hamburgers on the planet—though I'll admit to being biased, since I grew up eating them. Take a seat at the coun-

The Queen Mary

ter, and be sure to save room for a slice of the wonderful fruit pies. Late at night, the huge sandwiches and heart-warming soups at **Canter's Deli** (419 N. Fairfax Ave., 323/651-2030, open daily 24 hours) draw all kinds of night owls to a lively New York-style deli in the heart of the predominantly Jewish Fairfax District. Downtown, between Chinatown, historic Olvera Street, and the landmark Union Station, **Philippe The Original** (1001 N. Alameda St., 213/628-3781) serves famous French dip sandwiches in a classic workers' cafeteria, offering good food at impossibly low prices, with character to spare.

The usual array of information about hotels, restaurants, tickets to TV show tapings, and all other L.A.-area attractions is available through the **Los Angeles Tourism and Convention Board** (6801 Hollywood Blvd., 800/228-2452).

a surfer at the Huntington Beach Pier

Huntington Beach

Winding south and east from Long Beach, Hwy-1 continues along the coast past a series of natural marshlands and small-craft marinas. The first real point of interest is the town of **Huntington Beach** (pop. 189,992), one of the largest communities in Orange County. Incorporated in 1909 and developed by Henry Huntington as a stop along his legendary Pacific Electric "Red Car" interurban railway network, Huntington Beach is best known as one of the places where **surfing** really took off on the U.S. mainland. To attract Angelenos down to his new town, Huntington hired Hawaiians to demonstrate the sport, which at the time made use of huge solid wooden boards, 15 feet long and weighing around 150 pounds. Huntington Beach, especially around the pier, is still a very popular surfing spot—though contemporary surfers slice through the waves on high-tech foam-core boards, a third of the size of the original Hawaiian long boards. The history and culture of West Coast surfing, with examples of boards then and now (plus special collections highlighting surf movies and the creation of surf music by local heroes Leo Fender and Dick Dale), is recounted in the fantastic **International Surfing Museum** (411 Olive Ave., closed Mon., hours vary, $2), two blocks from the pier in the heart of the lively downtown business district.

Anaheim: Disneyland Resort

Like a little bit of middle America grafted onto the southern edge of Los Angeles, inland Orange County used to feel like a totally different world. Though the area's demographics have changed considerably in the past decade or two, becoming more a part of L.A.'s fast-paced, edg-

Angel Stadium

ily creative multiethnic stew, Orange County in the 1950s and 1960s was suburban America writ large—mostly white, mostly well-off, and absolutely, totally bland. In short, a perfect place to build the ultimate escapist fantasy, the self-proclaimed "Happiest Place on Earth," **Disneyland** (714/781-4565).

The major league baseball **Los Angeles Angels of Anaheim** play at **Angel Stadium** (2000 Gene Autry Way, 714/940-2000).

The phenomenon of Disneyland has been done to death by all sorts of social critics, but the truth is, it can be great fun—provided you visit out of season, get there early to avoid the crowds, and really immerse yourself in the extroverted, mindless joy of it all. (Being here in the company of appreciative 8 to 12-year-olds is probably the best way to maximize your enjoyment.)

If you haven't been before, or not for a while at any rate, here are some useful tidbits of information: Disneyland is 30 miles south of downtown L.A., right off I-5 in the city of Anaheim—you can see the Matterhorn from the freeway. The park is open daily; in summer, it remains open until midnight. Admission to the park, which includes all rides, costs around $100 per person per day.

Disneyland opened in 1955, when there was nothing surrounding it; in intervening years, an entire metropolis has grown up around it. In 2001 the park was joined by the much smaller, more grown-up-oriented **Disney California Adventure** theme park. This billion-dollar park has thrill rides like California Screamin', a 55-mph roller coaster, and the excellent Soarin' Over California motion simulator, offering an airborne tour of the Golden State from

Yosemite Falls to the Malibu beaches. The pièce de résistance is Cars Land, based on the animated Pixar film and featuring the 40-mph Radiator Springs Racers, which simulates a race down Route 66. Disney California Adventure is separate from Disneyland, but a Park Hopper pass allows entry into both.

The whole Disney ensemble includes an upscale resort-hotel complex, surrounded by motels and yet more motels, and it is well worth staying overnight so you can get an early start, go "home" for a while, then come back for the nightly fireworks show. A highly recommended place to stay is the **Sheraton Park Hotel** (1855 S. Harbor Blvd., 714/750-1811, $169 and up), a block from Disneyland, offering spacious modern rooms (and a nice pool), with free shuttles every half hour to and from Disneyland.

Richard Nixon Presidential Library

If you've already done the Disneyland thing, or just want a foil to the empty-headed fun, there is one other Orange County attraction you really shouldn't miss: the **Richard Nixon Presidential Library** (18001 Yorba Linda Blvd., 714/993-5075, daily, $11.95 adults), 10 miles northeast of Disneyland off Hwy-90. The library is built on the very ground where the former president was born in 1913; it's also where he and his wife, Pat, are buried, side by side next to the restored Craftsman-style bungalow where Nixon grew up. No matter what your feelings are toward him, the spare-no-expense displays do a fascinating job of putting his long career into the distorted perspective you'd expect from the only president ever forced to resign from office. Highlights are many, such as the pictures of the pumpkin patch where Whittaker Chambers concealed the microfilm that Nixon used to put Alger Hiss in prison as a Communist spy, next to photos of Nixon and JFK as chummy freshman U.S. senators sharing sleeping compartments on a train. The best-selling item in the gift shop? Photographs of Nixon greeting Elvis Presley, also available as mousepads, china cups, and fridge magnets.

Newport Beach

Back on the coast, if you want to get a sense of what wealthy Orange Countians do to enjoy themselves, spend some time along the clean white strands of **Newport Beach.** Located at the southern edge of Los Angeles's suburban sprawl, Newport started life in 1906 as an amusement park and beach resort at the southern end of the L.A. streetcar lines. Since then thousands of Angelenos have spent summer weekends at the **Balboa Pavilion,** at the southern tip of the slender Balboa peninsula, where the Fun Zone preserves a few remnants of the pre-video game amusements—a Ferris wheel, a merry-go-round, and those odd Pokerino games in which you win prizes by rolling rubber balls into a series of numbered holes. If you have some spare time, Newport is also a good base for taking the unforgettable cruise across the water to **Catalina Island,** a semi-tropical paradise 26 miles off the coast.

Midway along the peninsula, near 23rd Street, Newport Pier is flanked by another holdout from the old days: the dory fleet. For more than a century, small boats have set off from the beach here (often around midnight, landing back around 7am) to catch rock cod and more exotic fish, which are sold fresh off the boats at an outdoor market right on the sands.

A mile southeast of Balboa Pavilion, next to the breakwater at the very eastern end of Balboa peninsula, **The Wedge** is one of the world's most popular and challenging bodysurfing spots, with well-formed waves often twice as high as anywhere else on the coast.

To return to Hwy-1 from Balboa Peninsula, you can either backtrack around the harbor or ride the **Balboa Island Ferry,** which shuttles you and your car from the pavilion across the harbor past an amazing array of sailboats, power cruisers, and waterfront homes.

Crystal Cove State Park

Midway between Newport and Laguna Beaches, amidst the ever-encroaching Orange County sprawl, **Crystal Cove State Park** (949/494-3539, daily dawn-dusk, $15 per car) protects one of Southern California's finest chunks of coastline. With three miles of sandy beaches and chaparral-covered bluff lined by well-marked walking trails, it's a fine place to enjoy the shoreline without the

Crystal Cove State Park

commercial trappings. Originally home to Native Americans, the land here was later part of Mission San Juan Capistrano and, until 1979 when the state bought it, the massive Irvine Ranch, which once covered most of Orange County.

The main parking area for Crystal Cove is at **Reef Point** near the south end of the park, where there are bathrooms and showers plus excellent tide pools and a fine beach. You can stay overnight at **Crystal Cove Beach Cottages** (949/497-0900 or 800/444-7275, $42 and up), a well-preserved collection of 1930s-1950s beach bungalows. There is also a large section of the park inland from Hwy-1, through the oakland glade of **Moro Canyon,** which gives a vivid sense of Orange County's rapidly vanishing natural landscape.

Laguna Beach

Compared with much of Orange County, **Laguna Beach** (pop. 24,100) is a relaxed and enjoyable place. Bookstores, cafés, and galleries reflect the town's beginnings as an artists' colony, but while the beach and downtown area are still very attractive, the surrounding hills have been covered by some of the world's ugliest tracts of "executive homes."

During the annual summertime **Pageant of the Masters** (949/487-6582 or 800/487-3378, $20-158), Laguna Beach residents re-create scenes from classical and modern art by forming living tableaux, standing still as statues in front of painted backdrops. Proceeds go to good causes. It's a popular event, so get tickets well in advance.

Right across Hwy-1 from the down-town shopping district, which is full of pleasant cafés and a wide range of art galleries, Laguna's main beach (called simply **Main Beach**) is still the town's main draw, with a boardwalk, some vol-leyball courts, and a guarded swim-ming beach with showers.

Many other fine but usually less crowded and quieter beaches are reach-able from Cliff Drive, which winds north of downtown Laguna past cove after untouched cove; follow the signs reading Beach Access.

Laguna Beach has a number of nice places to eat. One place worth search-

tableau from Laguna Beach's Pageant of the Masters

ing out is the small **Taco Loco** (640 S. Coast Hwy., 949/497-1635), at the south end of the downtown strip, where the ultra-fresh Mexican food includes your choice of three or four different sea-food tacos, from shark to swordfish, in daily-changing specials from about $2 each.

Places to stay are expensive, averaging around $150 a night, and include the beachfront **Laguna Riviera** (825 S. Coast Hwy., 949/494-1196). At the top end of the scale, the **Montage** (30801 S. Coast Hwy., 866/271-6953, $595 and up) has everything you could want from a hotel.

South of Laguna Beach, Hwy-1 follows the coast for a final few miles before joining up with the I-5 freeway for the 65-mile drive into San Diego.

San Juan Capistrano

Of the 21 missions along the California coast, **Mission San Juan Capistrano** (949/234-1300, daily, $9 adults) has been the most ro-manticized. When the movement to restore the missions and pre-serve California's Spanish colonial past was at its apogee in the late 1930s, its main theme tune was Leon René's "When the Swallows Come Back to Capistrano," popularizing the legend that these birds return from their winter migration every St. Joseph's Day, March 19. After wintering in Goya, Argentina, they do come back to Capistrano, along with several thousand tourists, but the swallows

Mission San Juan Capistrano

are just as likely to reappear a week before or a week after—whenever the weather warms up, really.

The mission, which has lovely, bougainvillea-filled gardens, stands at the center of the small, eponymously named town, a short detour inland along I-5 from the coast. Besides the birds, the main attractions include the small **chapel,** the last surviving church where the beatified Father Serra said mass, widely considered the oldest intact church and perhaps the oldest building of any kind in California, and the ruins of the massive **Great Stone Church,** a finely carved limestone structure that collapsed in an earthquake in 1812, just six years after its completion. Many visitors to the chapel are terminally ill patients saying prayers to St. Peregrine, the patron saint of cancer patients.

To get a sense of the huge scale of the Great Stone Church, a church patterned after the fallen building has been constructed behind the mission and now serves as the official mission church, open to visitors except during religious services. Across the street from this church, Mission Basilica, a Michael Graves-designed local **library** gives an intriguing postmodern take on the mission style.

The Coach House (33157 Camino Capistrano, 949/496-8930), two miles south of the mission, is one of Southern California's best small clubs for listening to live music.

San Clemente

At the southern tip of coastal Orange County, **San Clemente** marks the midway point between San Diego and Los Angeles. A sleepy beachside community, with frequent Amtrak train service and a nicely undulating stretch of old US-101 (El Camino Real) running through its heart, San Clemente is probably best known as the site of La Casa Pacifica, the one-time "Western White House" of former president Richard Nixon, who lived here following his election in 1968 and during his impeachment in the mid-1970s. The white-walled, mission-style house at the south end of Avenida del Presidente (the western frontage road to I-5) is more easily visible from the beach below, though the 25 acres of trees have grown up to obscure it in recent years.

Within a quick walk uphill from the handful of cafés and bars on and around the pier, **Beachcomber Motel** (949/492-5457, $135 and up) is a tidy, old-fashioned motor-court motel, facing onto the open ocean. San Clemente also has a burger place, **Rider's Club Cafe** (1701 N. El Camino Real, 949/388-3758, closed Mon.), in the mission-style downtown business district.

Mission San Luis Rey de Francia

South of San Clemente, the northwest corner of San Diego County is taken up by the U.S. Marines Corps's massive **Camp Pendleton** training base, which fills 125,000 acres, running for 17 miles along the coast and about 15 miles inland. (The base motto is "No Beach out of Reach"). Camp Pendleton is the largest undeveloped section of the Southern California coast.

In the sun-bleached hills above the blue Pacific, four miles east of the ocean off the I-5 along Hwy-76, **Old Mission San Luis Rey de Francia** (daily, $5 adults) was the largest and among the most successful of the California missions. Its lands have been taken over by Camp Pendleton, and most of the outbuildings have disappeared, but the stately church at the heart of the complex survives in fine condition, worth a look for the blue-tinted dome atop the bell tower and for the haunting carved stone skull that looks down from the cemetery gate.

A long but worthwhile detour inland from San Luis Rey brings you to one of the least visited but perhaps most evocative of all

the California missions, **Mission San Antonio de Pala** (760/742-3317, closed Mon.-Tues., $2 adults). Located on the Pala Indian Reservation, 20 miles east of San Luis Rey along Hwy-76, then another 100 yards north along a well-marked side road, Mission San Antonio de Pala is the only California mission still serving its original role of preaching to the native people, and it gives an unforgettable impression of what California's mission era might have been like.

Oceanside

At the southern edge of 125,000-acre Marine Corps Base Camp Pendleton, **Oceanside** (pop. 164,500) is one of the largest cities between Los Angeles and San Diego, but it offers few tourist attractions—apart from a long fishing pier and guided tours of Camp Pendleton's amphibious-assault training exercises. But if you're in the mood to shop for camouflage gear, watch the muscle cars cruise Hill Street, get a $5 G.I. Joe haircut, or drink beer with a gang of young recruits, this is the right place.

Some of the best views of the Southern California coastline can be had from the windows of the frequent Coaster commuter trains, which run right along the shore between Oceanside and downtown San Diego.

Oceanside is also home to one of the last survivors of the old, pre-Interstate, Coast Highway businesses: The **101 Café** (631 S. Coast Hwy., 760/722-5220) has been open for classic road food since 1928. It often hosts classic car rallies and generally glows with neon-lit nostalgia. Other, more retro-minded All-American roadside favorites include the **Breakfast Club Diner** (228 N. Coast Hwy., 760/722-3124) and **Ruby's Diner** (760/433-7829), at the far end of the Oceanside Pier.

South from Oceanside, all the way to San Diego, a very pleasant alternative to the often-clogged I-5 is the old alignment of US-101, now signed as County Road S21 (and occasionally, Coast Highway 101). Slower than the freeway but still in regular use, the old road is now the main drag of quaint beachfront towns like Carlsbad, Leucadia, Encinitas, and Del Mar. If you have the time, it's a great drive, in sight of the ocean for most of the way.

Carlsbad: La Costa and Legoland

Named for the European spa town of Karlsbad, in Bohemia of what's now the Czech Republic, **Carlsbad** (pop. 105,328) was established in the 1880s as a spa town and vacation resort. A few remnants of the historic resort area still survive along old US-101 in the center of town. A few flower and strawberry fields surround the town, surviving against the ever-expanding tide of sprawl. These days Carlsbad's spa-town heritage lives on at **La Costa**

Resort and Spa (760/438-9111, $299 and up), a 500-plus-room complex of luxurious rooms, health spas, golf courses, and tennis courts covering 400 acres of hills on the inland side of I-5.

Carlsbad's other main attraction is the first American outpost of the popular European children's theme park **Legoland** (760/918-5346, $78 adults, $68 children). Built out of millions of Lego bricks, and covering 128 acres above the Pacific Ocean, the park is divided up into multiple areas, including Miniland USA, where miniature landscapes mod-

model of San Francisco made entirely from Lego blocks

eled on New York, New Orleans, New England, and Southern California have all been constructed using more than 40 million of the trademark plastic bricks.

South Carlsbad State Beach (760/438-3143, $12 per car), three miles south of town, is one of the nicest and most popular places to camp on the Southern California coast, with its spacious **campsites** ($35-50) with hot showers spread out along a sandstone bluff above a broad beach. However, swimming can be dangerous because of strong riptides. If you don't want to camp or pay the parking fee, leave your car at the park entrance, which is well marked on a surviving stretch of the old US-101 highway.

Del Mar and Torrey Pines

Most of the time, **Del Mar** (pop. 4,161) is a sleepy little upscale suburb of San Diego, with big houses backing onto more than two miles of fine beach. But in late summer, it comes to life for the thoroughbred racing season at beautiful **Del Mar racetrack,** built by Hollywood types like Bing Crosby and seen in *The Grifters* and many other Hollywood movies and TV shows. The waves here are well suited to bodysurfing, but the sands can be hard to reach in summer because of a lack of parking—weekdays it's less of a problem.

South along the Camino Del Mar coast road from Del Mar, hang-gliders, tide-poolers, surfers, and beachcombers flock to the nearly 2,000 acres of bluffs and beaches protected in **Torrey Pines State Natural Reserve.** Named for the long-needled pines that

San Diego

Set along a huge Pacific Ocean harbor at the southwestern corner of the country just a few miles from the Mexican border, San Diego embodies the Southern California ideal. Around the turn of the 20th century, it rivaled Los Angeles as a boomtown based on wild real estate speculation, but while L.A. continued to expand by leaps and bounds, San Diego grew comparatively slowly. Instead of Hollywood glamour, San Diego's economy has long been based on the U.S. Navy, as evidenced by the massive former USS *Midway* moored right downtown. (San Diego successfully mixed its military and Hollywood influences in the movie *Top Gun*.) Despite a metropolitan population of more than 3 million people, San Diego still feels small and anything but urban.

The main things to see in San Diego are in **Balboa Park,** a lushly landscaped 1,200-acre spread on downtown's northeast edge, which was largely laid out and constructed as part of the 1915 Panama-California Exposition celebrating the completion of the Panama Canal. The many grand buildings, all built in gorgeous Spanish Revival style by architect

Balboa Park

Bertram Goodhue, have been preserved in marvelous condition and now house sundry museums, ranging from automobiles to fine art to a functioning replica of Shakespeare's Globe Theatre.

Balboa Park is also home to the **San Diego Zoo** (619/231-1515, daily, $46 adults), one of the largest and most popular in the world with over 4,000 animals kept in settings that simulate their natural habitats. You can see koalas and komodo dragons, panda bears and polar bears, plus gorillas, giraffes—you name it, if it's anywhere outside in the wild, it'll be here amidst the zoo's lushly landscaped 100 acres.

The **San Diego Padres** (619/795-5000) play at very popular, retro-modern Petco Park, right downtown in the Gaslamp Quarter.

San Diego Zoo

PRACTICALITIES

The city of San Diego bends diagonally around its natural harbor, which makes orientation occasionally confusing. The main airport, Lindbergh Field, is on the waterfront just northwest of downtown—and has one of the swiftest final approaches of any urban American airport. Because it is small and relatively compact, San Diego is easy to get around. Downtown is walkable, and on a bike you could see most everything in a day. Buses operated by **San Diego Metropolitan Transit** (619/557-4555) fan out from downtown, while the light rail **San Diego Trolley** runs south from downtown to the Mexican border.

Though you may feel the need to duck when planes land at nearby Lindbergh Field, for breakfast try the **Hob Nob Hill** (2271 First Ave., 619/239-8176), a classic 1940s coffee shop with great pecan waffles. For more all-American fare, head west to Ocean Beach, where **Hodad's** (5010 Newport Ave., 619/224-4623), a great old burger joint, awaits you. San Diego's Old Town historic park holds some good old-school Mexican places, like the **Old Town Mexican Café** (2489 San Diego Ave., 619/297-4330). In Balboa Park, soak up San Diego's Spanish Revival splendor while enjoying a meal at **The Prado** (619/557-9441) in the original House of Hospitality.

Places to stay are generally modern, clean, and comfortable, though rates vary with seasons (and conventions). For top-of-the-line accommodations, or just to appreciate the historic architecture, head to the wonderful old **Hotel del Coronado** (1500 Orange Ave., 619/435-6611, $289 and up), across the bridge from downtown on Coronado Island. Rising up in turreted glory, this fabulously grand, Victorian-era resort hotel still caters, as it always has, to the four-star trade. It has been seen in many movies, including the great Peter O'Toole flick *The Stunt Man.* It's also where England's King Edward VIII is rumored to have first met the femme fatale who inspired him to give up his throne: Mrs. Wallis Simpson, whose first husband was first commanding officer of the local Navy base. The cheapest beds are at the **HI-San Diego Downtown Hostel** (521 Market St., 619/525-1531, $30 and up per person), in the historic downtown Gaslamp Quarter, or the hip **500 West Hotel** (500 West Broadway, 619/234-5252, $49 and up), a boutique restoration of a 1920s YMCA. For more comfort and character, try **The Sofia Hotel** (150 W. Broadway, 619/234-9200, $139 and up), a restored 1920s hotel. For surfer-friendly (and pet-friendly!) accommodations near Ocean Beach and Point Loma, try the **Ocean Villa Inn** (5142 W. Point Loma Blvd., 619/224-3481, $99 and up).

The best range of information is available from the **San Diego International Visitor Information Center** (1140 N. Harbor Dr., 619/236-1212), on the waterfront near the massive USS *Midway* battleship.

A Torrey Pine, San Diego, Cal.—9

grow naturally only here, the reserve is crisscrossed by hiking trails leading down steep ravines between the bluffs and the sands. Besides hang-gliders, Torrey Pines is prime air space for remote-controlled model gliders, which float gracefully in the nearly constant onshore breeze. The primary launching spot is the small city park at the south end of the reserve.

Overlooking the Pacific from atop a bluff at the south end of the reserve, the **Salk Institute** is one of the world's most important centers for research in the life sciences. Founded by the late Jonas Salk, designed by Louis Kahn, and modeled in part on the gardens of the Alhambra in Granada, the institute is open for **tours** (858/453-4100, Mon.-Fri. 11:45am, $15 donation).

Stretching inland and south from the Salk Institute, the hills are covered with faceless business parks around the spacious campus of **University of California at San Diego** (UCSD), beyond which spreads La Jolla and the greater San Diego area. On campus, learn all about local marine biology at the **Birch Aquarium** (858/534-3474, $17 adults) of UCSD's Scripps Institution of Oceanography, from where you can amble along the shore to lovely La Jolla.

La Jolla

The wealthiest and most desirable part of San Diego, **La Jolla** sits along the coast northwest of the city proper, gazing out over azure coves to the endless Pacific. Besides the gorgeous scenery, great surfing (head to **Windansea Beach** for the best waves), beachcombing, and skin diving, a big draw here is the recently renovated **Museum of Contemporary Art** (700 Prospect St., 858/454-3541, closed Wed., $10 adults), overlooking the ocean. Tons of good cafés and restaurants have long made La Jolla an all-around great day out, suiting all budgets—especially those with no upper limit.

Start the day off right at La Jolla's **The Cottage** (7702 Fay Ave., 858/454-8409), where delicious food (including a divine buttermilk coffee cake) is served up on a

sunny patio. For an unforgettable, swaddled-in-luxury SoCal experience, stay the night at the elegant, Craftsman-style **The Lodge at Torrey Pines** (11480 N. Torrey Pines Rd., 858/453-4420, $400 and up), a modern re-creation of California's turn-of-the-20th-century Golden Age.

At **Belmont Park** (3146 Mission Blvd., 858/228-9283), west of Mission Bay, the Giant Dipper wooden roller coaster survives as the sole remnant of a 1920s beachfront amusement park.

Driving San Diego

From La Jolla south, the US-101 highway is pretty well buried by the I-5 freeway. Old US-101 can still be followed, however, by following Pacific Highway past Mission Bay and Lindbergh Field toward San Diego Bay, where it becomes Harbor Drive—where the light rail San Diego Trolley now runs.

Index

Photo and Illustration Credits

All vintage postcards, photographs and maps in this book from the private collection of Jamie Jensen, unless otherwise credited. Photos © Jamie Jensen: pages 18, 20, 41, 53, 56, 58, 113, 135.

United States Quarter-Dollar Coin Images

State quarter-dollar coin images from the United States Mint. Used with permission.

United States Postage Stamps

All postage stamps © United States Postal Service. All rights reserved. Used with permission. Written authorization from the Postal Service is required to use, reproduce, post, transmit, distribute, or publicly display these images. Pages 8, 28, 50 Greetings from America Series Stamp Designs © 2002 United States Postal Service.

The following images were sourced from www.123rf.com:

7 © Andrew Zarivny, 9 © Travis Manley, 12 © Steve Estvanik, 18 (bottom) © Harry Hu, 31 © Steve Estvanik, 44 © Shirley Palmer, 47 © Jill Battaglia, 51 © iofoto, 72 (top) © Julia Nelson, 78 © Mariusz Jurgielewicz, 84 © Mariusz Jurgielewicz, 99 © Mariusz Jurgielewicz, 102 © Mike Norton, 109 © Charles Shapiro, 120 © Byron Moore, 124 © Stranger-View, 125 © Andrew Kazmierski, 126 © Randy Hines, 101 © Kan Khampanya, 132 © Wayne Geisler, 136 (bottom) © Deepa Vaswani, 136 (top) © Andrew Zarivny.

Public Domain images:

The following images are in the public domain because one of the following applies:
· The work is a work of a U.S. government soldier or employee, taken or made during the course of the person's official duties. As a work of the U.S. federal government, the image is in the public domain.
· The work was published in the United States between 1923 and 1977 and without a copyright notice. Unless its author has been dead for several years, it is copyrighted in jurisdictions that do not apply the rule of the shorter term for US works, such as Canada (50 p.m.a.), Mainland China (50 p.m.a., not Hong Kong or Macao), Germany (70 p.m.a.), Mexico (100 p.m.a.), Switzerland (70 p.m.a.), and other countries with individual treaties.
· The copyright has expired, often because the first publication of the image occurred prior to January 1, 1923.
· The copyright holder of the work has released the work into the public domain. This applies worldwide. In some countries this may not be legally possible; if so: The copyright holder grants anyone the right to use the work for any purpose, without any conditions, unless such conditions are required by law.
· The work is a postage stamp published before 1978.
See http://copyright.cornell.edu/resources/publicdomain.cfm for further explanation.

5 shield Courtesy of SPUI/Wikimedia Commons; 31 stamp courtesy of United States Postal Service; 80 (bottom) Courtesy of Two+two=4/Wikimedia Commons; 87 (photo) Courtesy of Jacob Kearns/Wikimedia Commons; 101 Courtesy of Scott Frier/Nikon/U.S. Fish & Wildlife Service; 117 and 118 (top) digital files Courtesy of Kevin Roe Collection; 127 Courtesy of HerSilverHammer/Wikimedia Commons; 128 Courtesy Nixon Presidential Library and Museum, original taken July 9, 1972; 129 Courtesy of Ulfer/Wikimedia Commons.